One Man's Bath

One Man's Bath

Canon Richard Askew

Millstream Books

Dedicated to my wife, Margaret,
my companion on pilgrimage

cover illustrations:
(front) The author shows off the Abbey's view of Bath from high on
its northern wall during the recent restoration.
(rear) Over 1,000 members of the congregation swarm into Abbey
Churchyard to hear the Bishop deliver his Easter message
from the West Front gallery.

First published in 2000 by
Millstream Books, 18 The Tyning, Bath BA2 6AL

Set in Times New Roman
Printed in Great Britain by The Jensen Press, Yeovil

© Richard Askew 2000

ISBN 0 948975 62 8

British Library Cataloguing-in-Publication Data:
a catalogue record for this book is available from The British Library

Introduction

"Gee", said the American visitor, gazing up at the Abbey's West Front from the Churchyard, "you've sure got an extensive facility here".

I had never thought about the Abbey in quite those terms before but the more I reflected on it, the more I recognised the accuracy of the description. The Abbey truly is an extensive facility. Spatially it is vast, drawing the eye upwards into the soothing harmony of its fan vaulting. But it extends downwards too, through the layer cake of its history, revealing to us, in turn, the floor of the preceding Norman cathedral; next showing us the traces of the Saxon church known to the Brothers of St Peter and to King Edgar; and finally landing with a bump in the bargain basement – probably a Roman supermarket or similar, set in its cobbled marketplace.

But the Abbey extends outwards too, its tendrils wrapped around many aspects of Bath's life. There was a time when the Abbey, along with the hot baths, constituted the *raison d'être* of Bath itself. The Abbey filled one quadrant of the medieval city with its grounds and outbuildings and must have dominated the economy of the other three quadrants.

Six hundred and forty memorial plaques on the Abbey's walls testify to the fact that in the 18th century people flocked from all over the kingdom to take the waters, deemed to be a sovereign remedy for all ills; the sheer number of the memorials in fact underscores the sad inability of Bath's waters to cure anybody of anything very much: there are some 4,000 such 'failures' buried beneath the Abbey's floor. To put it as delicately as possible – in those days, before refrigeration, you were buried where you dropped. Sheridan, the 18th-century dramatist, in his play *The Rivals*, comments that there is "snug lying in the Abbey".

Today the Abbey is not just a haven for dead Bathonians, but one of the pivotal points of Bath's life, and a major element in Bath's tourist appeal. Drawing one third of a million visitors a year, in Bath it rates second for popularity after the Roman Baths, and nationally is one of England's two most visited parish churches. Culturally, in a city that lacks a purpose-built concert hall, the Abbey provides a major auditorium, hosting over 50 musical events a year, over and above its own worship.

Bath's Abbey, therefore, provides an excellent starting point from which to explore Bath, past, present and future; and that is what this book seeks to do. Using the Abbey as our base we shall tunnel out into the life of one of England's most intriguing communities. We shall try to discover in the contemporary city some of the visible traces of the city of past centuries hidden beneath our feet. Bath's fourth dimension is its history, and it is never far beneath the surface.

I want to emphasise, however, that this book is what it says it is – one man's Bath. It does not seek to be either a comprehensive guide or a complete history; it is simply a distillation of ten years of impressions and experiences during which time I have had the joyful privilege of serving as the Abbey's Rector. I hope I may be forgiven if this highly individualistic glimpse of Bath is seen through the Abbey's stained glass windows: perhaps this may be no bad thing, for the building is indeed "an extensive facility".

1 In the Beginning

A medieval legend, as misty as the steam rising from the hot baths, records the shadowy figure of Prince Bladud. Bladud, so the story goes, was expelled from court by his father, King Lud, after catching leprosy while studying at the University of Athens.

On being exiled from high society Bladud displayed a hardy independence of mind by getting himself a job as a swineherd. Sadly, however, his pigs became infected with his own dire disease. Wandering disconsolately one day with his herd of scrofulous swine, Bladud arrived at a hill overlooking our hot springs. His charges, in their insatiable quest for acorns, dashed down the hill to disappear into a patch of marshland, which, unaccountably, appeared to be steaming hot. No doubt the pigs had been attracted to the warmth, but to Bladud's amazement he saw that their sores and scabs had been healed. Rushing into the hot mud after them, Bladud himself was also cleansed. Reinstated as heir to the throne, he ought to have lived happily ever after: that is the way his story deserves to end. However, not content with one miracle, he essayed another by experimenting with winged flight. He crashed to his doom, having previously fathered a yet more tragic figure – King Lear.

Decorative acorns in the Circus recall the legend of Bladud's pigs – a profitable fiction for Bath.

This pleasing fable, set comfortably back in the 9th century BC, comes to us through an imaginative Welsh priest, Geoffrey of Monmouth, who in 1185 completed a fanciful history of pre-Conquest Britain, allegedly based on a 'very old book' from Brittany. What this chronicle lacked in historical accuracy it amply compensated for in commercial utility: the potent myth of the therapeutic virtue of Bath's hot springs had been endowed with respectable antiquity. It was in time to make the city's fortune. No wonder Bladud lives on today in Bath's street names, and his pigs' acorns adorn its architecture.

A less colourful, if more verifiable, account of Bath's origins tells of the great military road constructed by the Romans shortly after their invasion of these islands in 43 AD. Now called the *Fosse Way*, it linked Exeter with Lincoln, and served as an early frontier line in the first days of the occupation. On the south-east side of the road lay a rich civilisation that stretched back to the Mediterranean basin; to the north-west, nothing but uncharted barbarism: 'here be dragons' – and Welsh dragons at that. This great road crossed the Avon somewhere in Bath, probably near the present-day Cleveland Bridge, and the crossing point became the focus for the first Roman settlement of Bath – a rash of artisan roadside development in the Walcot area, much the same as we see today.

The significance of the thermal springs was very soon appreciated and exploited. Before the coming of the Romans the local Celts had responded to the wonder of the ceaseless flow of hot water by crediting it to their deity, Sulis, and had accordingly built a shrine. The invading Roman forces deliberately drove a roadway through the centre of this shrine – "the equivalent", as Professor Barry Cunliffe puts it, "to building a motorway through Wells Cathedral precinct!" Twenty years later, more diplomatic administrators equated Sulis with their own Minerva and constructed a magnificent temple and sanctuary to the honour of a conflated Sulis-Minerva. Perhaps this was a conciliatory move in the wake of Boudicca's dangerous revolt of AD6O. The development of the bathing establishment, executed with great engineering skill, followed swiftly in the last decades of the 1st century. It became famous throughout Britain and beyond, and remained in use for some 400 years, drawing visitors from across the Roman world. Bath's tourism industry was born.

Yet right from the start there was more to it than simply a sybaritic wish to bask in the comfort of endless warm water. The hot springs were seen as not only highly convenient but also as awesome, the manifestation of divine power and a source of healing. That was why the Romans married up Minerva with Sulis, for Minerva included curative powers within her portfolio.

In the hot water bubbling up from the Sacred Spring, the Britons saw Sulis at work and the Romans glimpsed their goddess Minerva.

To address Minerva, the visitor (or was he a pilgrim?) went not just to the temple, but also to the hot baths, where a prayer request could be inscribed on a pewter sheet, rolled up and entrusted to the waters. Local residents too consigned all their concerns, both great and trivial, to these sheets, just as contemporary Bathonians consign theirs to the correspondence columns of the *Bath Chronicle*. 1900 years later, these pewter sheets were to be unrolled and deciphered by the archaeologists. A number of these prayers, or curses, can be inspected in the Roman Baths. They provide a fascinating insight into what agitated the average Roman Bathonian – family disputes, the seduction of a girlfriend, the theft of a bath towel.

If the curses give us an insight into people's daily pre-occupations, archaeology also traces for us the development of a compact community within walls which underlie the city's medieval fortifications (still to be seen at some points today).

The resident population would have been small, largely contained within an area of 23 acres. The city lived to some extent by its position on the Fosse Way, but primarily as a centre for recreation and pilgrimage for those drawn by the allure of the hot springs.

The terrifying Gorgon's head, glaring down from the Temple pediment, is a synthesis of a Roman theme and Celtic craftsmanship.

The sense of awe generated by the sight of hot water welling up from the earth was deliberately enhanced by the builders of the adjacent temple. At the centre of its pediment, frowning down on the worshipper, they set the fearsome head of a Gorgon. Discovered in 1790, this head is the most significant carving to be found in the whole baths complex. The inspiration is clearly Roman: the execution of the face, with its curling locks, terrifying gaze, and ferocious moustaches, is as clearly Celtic. The sculptor has converted the Gorgon – a female in Roman mythology – into a fearsome male visage. A syncretism of both art and religion had been achieved to mark the awesomeness of the place and to strike a shaft of dread into the hearts of those who came in search of the healing powers of the place.

It is interesting to note the ingredient of terror in the worship of the ancient world. I remember encountering a much larger Gorgon's head amongst the ruins of the Greek temple at Didyma in Turkey. The effect on a simple suppliant of encountering such a terrifying visage frowning down from the temple's pediment may well be imagined. There is a proper sense of awe in our approach to God, but it should not need to be artificially induced.

This, then, was how the inhabitants of Aquae Sulis – "waters of Sulis" – viewed their gods up to the time when a strange new sect entered the life of the city, destined to shake the established

The Abbey rises above the place where Sulis and Minerva were once worshipped.

orthodoxies to destruction. This sect would eventually change the, face of Bath and, some 1200 years later, bring about the construction of the great church that is today the city centre's most majestic architectural landmark.

2 From Twilight To Dawn

A great mystery hangs over the ending of the Roman period of our history. Did the Roman army depart tidily, in the manner of much of our own withdrawal from empire, marching out on the appointed day behind the legionary band, with eagles held aloft, leaving the locals to squabble over the pickings? Or were they instead ousted in a piecemeal way by fresh waves of invaders breaking through the defences of the Saxon Shore? Or did Romano-Celtic communities survive, not to be massacred but eventually to be assimilated?

Facts are few and far between. In the year 410 the Emperor Honorius, hard pressed by barbarian incursions from central Europe, wrote from Rome to the cities in Britannia telling them that henceforth they could expect no more help. From now on they were on their own, left to fight off attacks from the continent. In the Roman twilight that ensued it is fascinating to conjecture just how much survived in terms of both the architectural and social fabric of the country.

At Bath a dwindling glow of Roman civilisation survived for at least a further century and a half after Honorius' bleak communiqué, before the city, along with Gloucester and Cirencester, fell to the advancing Saxon warlords, previously held in check by a Celtic victory at 'Mount Badon' – an unidentified site thought by many to be near Bath. During that twilight period, Bath shed much of its former glory and must have been a sad community, riven with internal dissensions, faced with the decline of its population and the decay of the great bathing establishment, and, above all, overshadowed by the threat of attack from the east and from the south.

Reference has already been made to the prayers and curses written out on pewter sheets and tossed into the Sacred Spring for the attention of the goddess Minerva. One such sheet was inscribed about the year 350 by an aggrieved citizen, one Annianus, who had suffered a robbery. He asks the lady goddess for due retribution on the culprit "whether pagan or Christian, whosoever, whether man or woman, whether boy or girl, whether slave or free, has stolen from me, Annianus, in the morning, six silver pieces from my purse". His indignation remained set in

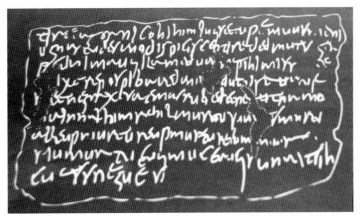

The facsimile of Annianus' curse: inscribed on pewter c.350AD, it gives us the first written use of the word 'Christian' in Britain.

pewter, known only to him and the goddess Minerva (and no doubt his wife heard a lot about it too), until Professor Barry Cunliffe's 1970s' excavations in the King's Bath uncovered his passionate plea. The tablet may be seen today in the Roman Baths Museum, and, in replica, in the Abbey's Heritage Vaults.

The significant fact about this inscription is its use of the word "Christian" – its first appearance in writing in this country. It implies the existence of a Christian community from as early as the mid-4th century. Archaeology produces another clue to support this conclusion. A memorial commemorating the repair of part of the pagan temple defaced by "impious hands" may perhaps record an early act of Christian iconoclasm. We can envisage within Bath's generally pagan culture the existence of a despised minority of Christians; some would argue that the situation is very similar today.

Alongside the crumbling pagan cults went the crumbling of the baths themselves. The Roman engineers, who had solved so many problems, were defeated by one challenge which was not to be finally overcome until the 1980s. The outflow drain from the Baths emptied through a channel leading to an aperture in the river wall, and thence into the river Avon. Every now and then the river flooded above the level of this outflow. The result would be a backing-up of flood water and mud into the baths and the temple area. All the engineers could do was to wait for the waters to recede

The flow of hot water, channelled here by the Romans from the Sacred Spring into the Great Bath, provides Bath's original raison d'être.

and then to begin the task of mopping up. Eventually money and energy to do this ran out. The mud was left triumphant, the baths abandoned and in time the great temple itself came crashing down.

The Saxons inherited this decayed glory after their success at the Battle of Dyrham in 577, avenging their previous repulse. Simple bucolic folk, they were baffled and amazed by what remained of the city's great buildings.

From a later date in the 8th century comes down to us a poem describing a Saxon reaction to the ruins of the baths: "wondrous is this masonry shattered by the Fates ... the buildings raised by giants are crumbling ... the roofs have collapsed ... the towers are in ruins and so these courts lie desolate and the structure of the dome with its red arches sheds its tiles. There stood courts of stone and a stream gushed forth in rippling floods of hot water. The wall enfolded within its bright bosom the whole place which contained the hot flood of the baths."

The author of this poem was most likely a monk from the Brothers of St Peter, whom we know to have been established in the city by the year 757. The monks, however, were not the first organised Christian presence in Bath. Already a century earlier a community of nuns had been set up in 675, the successors of those individual Roman Christians whose numbers perhaps included

Annianus' pickpocket. This community of nuns was headed by a Frankish Abbess, Berta, no doubt a formidable lady. At some point the nuns gave way to the Brothers (and women's ministry vanished on the site until the Abbey appointed its first woman deacon in 1992).

The monastic dedication to St Peter is commemorated in the present dedication of the Abbey. Somewhere down the centuries St Peter was joined by St Paul, and both our patrons gaze out benignly at Abbey Churchyard from their niches by the West Doors. With their complementary commitment to building up the Church and to spreading the faith, they are a source of inspiration for the Abbey's ministry today. Two years ago a party from the Abbey travelled on pilgrimage to Rome, where our patrons spent their final years and where they were martyred. We were privileged to be allowed to visit the excavations some metres under the floor of St Peter's. We entered the world of the 1st century as we walked along a narrow street flanked on either side by family tombs. At the end of this avenue of the dead we came to an undistinguished and anonymous grave containing a stone sarcophagus. On the inside of the sarcophagus, hidden from prying Vandal eyes, are carved the words: "Hic est Petrus". It was a profoundly moving moment for all of us as we mentally connected the bones which had been buried there with the little group of monks bearing his name and living out the Christian life in far-away Bath.

It is likely that these Christian communities established themselves where the Abbey now stands. In 1727 work-men digging drains in Stall Street discovered at the bottom of their trench a bronze head of Minerva. This head had been roughly severed and was found face down in the mud; the rest of the statue has never been found. Possibly it was a group of outraged Christians who at some

The head of the goddess Minerva, found face down in the mud under Stall Street in 1727. Deliberately thrown down, or laid to rest? (Photo by courtesy of the Roman Baths Museum)

15

stage had overthrown this symbol of a pagan past. Augustine, first Archbishop of Canterbury, on instructions from Pope Gregory, had laid down the principle that pagan temples should be demolished but their foundations should then be used to facilitate the construction of churches. This ruling satisfied the needs of both orthodoxy and economy. The evidence of three rounded stones suggests that the great temple of Minerva was confronted across the sacred enclosure by another smaller temple of circular construction known as a *tholos*. This would have stood beneath the west end of the present Abbey, where today they hand out the hymnbooks. It is probable that Bath's first purpose-built Christian church rose above the ruins of this *tholos*.

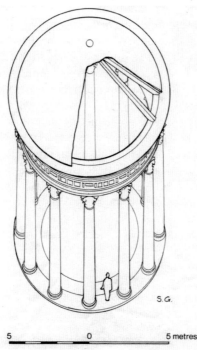

5   0   5 metres

The discovery of three large curved stones suggests that a circular temple, or tholos, *once stood within the west end of the Abbey. (Sketch by courtesy of Sheila Gibson)*

During the excavation of the Abbey's Heritage Vaults in 1993, on the south side of the church, the archaeologists dug deep beneath the floors of the 18th-century vaults, to discover many monastic burials. We recognised that some of these forefathers in the faith were Saxons by the manner of their interment – their bodies laid on a bed of charcoal, and their heads supported by stones to look upwards. Others had been members of the community in Norman times. Of the 30 skeletons uncovered, one was that of a woman who had died, at a relatively early age, early in the 13th century. Some hailed her

The Temple precinct, looking east. (By courtesy of the Roman Baths Museum)

The same view today, 14 feet above the Roman level.

discovery as early evidence for the ordination of women: the correct explanation of her presence is, no doubt, that she was a benefactress. Today, thanks to the Abbey's Friends, her bones lie in honoured state, visible beneath a sheet of glass.

Before that reburial could take place, her skeleton, together with those of the other 29, had to be taken to Bristol for carbon-dating. I gave my permission on condition that they should then be brought back to their original resting-place. In due course this happened and the vergers spent a macabre morning sorting a large pile of bones into separate plastic bags. They did their best but I suspect that there may be considerable embarrassment and confusion on the Day of Resurrection. Later that day I had invited a group of contemporary Benedictines from Downside Abbey to join us for an ecumenical service of reinterment. The Prior had accepted the proposal with enthusiasm and promised to send his best chanting monks for the occasion. We duly left the Abbey in procession, headed by the group of monks chanting psalms in Latin, to the puzzlement of the populace. Not to be outdone, I instructed my colleague at that time, a former professional singer, to render the finest *Nunc Dimittis* ever sung in the Church of England. With the upturned bathtub effect of the Vaults providing perfect acoustics, he excelled himself. Honours were judged to be equal when we adjourned for tea and a Bath bun.

Bath flourished in Saxon times as a vast, if loose-knit, estate with a number of different focal points. Gradually the town centre was again built up, and the city's economic importance is shown by the fact that the 10th century saw the operation of a mint as well as the growth of an important stone sculpture workshop. The 10th century also saw the revival of the monastery; Arch-bishop Dunstan's great 'Age of Reform' saw it reconstituted according to the Rule of St Benedict.

A scriptorium was established where the monks, forerunners of the photocopier, copied out the Gospels for use in local churches. One of them, Aelfricus, may still be seen in the Heritage Vaults, at work on a copy of the scriptures for Widcombe parish!

Bath's growing prosperity and importance, and its location as a frontier town between the two great Saxon kingdoms of Wessex and Mercia, made it the ideal location for a landmark event in our national history. In 957 Edgar had been elected King of a unified England: in 973 he legitimised his 16 years of peaceful rule by having himself crowned in the church which now stood on the bluff, looking down over the Avon valley. It was a joyful event of immense significance. *The Anglo-Saxon Chronicle* tells us: "Great joy had come to all on that blessed day which the children of men call and name the Day of Pentecost. There was assembled a crowd of priests, a great throng of learned monks". This gathering of the good and great included no less than two who were later

The coronation of King Edgar took place at Pentecost 973. "Mickle bliss" says one translation of the Anglo-Saxon Chronicle *"was enjoyed at Bath on that happy day".*

to be canonised as saints – the Archbishops Dunstan and Oswald: this record of sanctity within the congregation has not been equalled in recent years.

The service over which the Archbishops presided contained the elements of our present Coronation Service and marked the monarchy's sense of its need for divine commissioning.

This fact was to be celebrated 1,000 years later when Her Majesty Queen Elizabeth II visited the Abbey for a Service of Thanksgiving: a stone plaque in the nave commemorates this event.

With the choice of Bath as the site for Edgar's Coronation the city may be seen to have emerged from the Dark Ages into the clear light of its remarkable destiny.

3 From Coronation To Desolation

The crowning of Edgar marked a high point in the history of Bath and in the history of the country as a whole, now unified and no longer a conglomeration of separate Saxon kingdoms. The Viking menace still remained, however, and 30 years later disgruntled western princelings, betrayed by King Ethelred's unreadiness, had to gather in Bath to make their sullen submission to Swein, King of Denmark. Yet the next major threat was to come not from the north but from those Viking invaders of the French coast known to us as the Normans.

The shock waves of the Norman invasion hit Bath in 1088. William the Conqueror had died in the previous year, and discontented Norman knights in the region rose in revolt against his successor, William Rufus, sacking the city of Bath in the process. William put down the rebellion and appointed his own chaplain, John of Tours (John de Villula), as Bishop of Wells to keep an eye on things. John was an astute and able man, skilled in medicine as well as theology. He was greatly attracted by Bath and its therapeutic springs – by no means the last doctor to realise their commercial possibilities. Relying on the current policy of moving episcopal seats to the larger centres of population, he obtained permission in 1092 to migrate from Wells to Bath and henceforth styled himself "Bishop of Bath". He is on record as stating that he had no desire to live in obscurity in a mere village. His next move was to engineer the purchase of the city from the King – even in those days a snip at £500, paid in silver. The nature of this transaction is questionable: Britton's history quotes Matthew Paris as stating that John obtained the city "through anointing the King's hand with white ointment'.

The way was now clear for him to develop his plans for Bath. He set in motion a building programme to repair the destruction caused by the revolt, and above all he began to build a new church in place of the humbler structures of the Saxon monastery.

The new cathedral was enormous. The present Abbey is contained within the foundations of its nave alone, extending no further east than the original crossing. To this day the original pillars march some 8 feet below the present church, and may be seen at certain points through gratings in the floor. If today's Abbey still dominates the city centre, the former cathedral must have towered over the humble dwellings huddled around it. The three apses at its east end extended well out into what is now Orange Grove.

Along with this architectural aggrandisement John intended to upgrade the quality of the monastic community. Saxon monks were eased out in favour of French monks drawn from the new ruling class.

The cathedral under the carpet. An Abbey verger indicates the Norman columns of the old cathedral, still to be seen beneath the Abbey floor.

The Normans generally held the Saxon Church in low regard. An attempt had recently been made to strike Bath's own St Alphege from the calendar. Alphege, born around 953, after spending time as a monk at Deerhurst in Gloucestershire, had become Abbot of Bath a century before John de Villula arrived as its Bishop. Such was the impact of Alphege's rigorous spirituality that "the prominent citizens of the town immediately flooded to him, discovering the wounds of their souls to him and eagerly asking for counsel about heavenly things from him". Alphege left Bath to become Bishop of Winchester in 984 and Archbishop of Canterbury in 1005. There he was taken prisoner by the Danes and murdered by them at Greenwich during a drunken orgy, when he refused to exact the extortionate ransom they demanded – £3,000 – from the poor farmers of Kent. His heroic death had made him a national hero at the time.

The Norman attempts to deny his sanctity were rebuffed, however, by the Norman Archbishop Lanfranc, who, on the advice of St Anselm, declared that Alphege had been martyred for truth and justice, and therefore for God. Today St Alphege is commemorated in a special chapel dedicated to him in the Abbey with a graphic altar frontal depicting his heroic story.

Alphege had been reinstated just before John de Villula's arrival, and his name no doubt added lustre to the community and the great church being built for its use. Another figure, too, brought distinction to the Brothers of St Peter at this time – Adelard of Bath, who studied at the Abbey in the early years of the 12th century.

He can be justly acclaimed as England's first scientist, and Bath should make more of a fuss of him than it does (why not a Chair named in his honour at the University?).

Adelard's forte lay in his knowledge of Arabic, by which he was able to access Greek scientific thought, banned as heretical by the Church but greatly valued by Arab thinkers. Adelard translated his findings into Latin, the respectable *lingua franca*, and so made them accessible to Western thought. He literally put Bath on the map by devising an astrolabe and thus plotting the city's position with tolerable accuracy.

Our monastic ancestors in the faith were uncovered, and reverently reburied, in the cause of the Heritage Vaults excavations.

So began a golden age for the community at Bath, now termed 'Priory' as the Bishop had abrogated to himself the title of Abbot. This era was to last throughout the 12th century and into the 13th. The city's standing was likewise enhanced when King Richard, Coeur de Lion, desperate to raise funds to finance his crusading, sold Bath its Charter in 1189: a disreputable origin for an honour the city rightly deserved.

A monk called Aelfricus copied out one of the gospels for Widcombe parish and tells us so in his preface. His effigy is still at work.

Two factors brought the Priory's heyday to a close – an ugly piece of ecclesiastical politics in the 13th century and a devastating outbreak of plague in the 14th century. The clergy at Wells, rankling from the removal of their Bishop, plotted to lure him back to their small Somerset town. They achieved success in 1245 when the Pope, anticipating the great tradition of Anglican compromise, declared the See to be a joint one, with the double title of "Bath and Wells"; and that is what it is called to this day. The centre of gravity moved decisively to Wells at this time, where Bishop Joscelin had continued the construction of the vast cathedral. In this unseemly episcopal tug-of-war, Wells has triumphed – for the time being.

Nowadays the Bishop by no means ignores Bath Abbey but uses it for episcopal occasions at our end of the Dioceses. One such was a wave of mission through the diocesan area, launched by a service to be repeated on the same day at the three centres of Wells, Bath and Taunton. Our two Bishops and a visiting Zambian Bishop were to preside at each service. This feat of ubiquity could only be accomplished by the use of a helicopter. The episcopal whirlybird duly deposited its prelatical party on the Recreation Ground, whence a car sped them to the Abbey. Bishop Jim preached a powerful sermon and then made a swift exit, once again to be carried up to heaven. But one vital item he left behind – his sermon notes. It gave me great pleasure to instruct my colleague: "Take a taxi and follow that helicopter".

Such immediate episcopal epiphanies were not possible in the 13th century, and, with the departure of the Bishop to the countryside, the heart went out of the Bath community. A century later matters moved sharply from bad to worse. In 1348 plague struck, and the parochial clergy moving about their pastoral duties, or monks living closely in community, appear to have been decimated by this scourge. The monastic community, which in 1206 had numbered 41, totalled just 17 in 1377. Clearly the losses caused by the disease had not been made good, possibly because the first stirrings of Reformation thought were already making men hesitate about a monastic vocation.

Throughout this whole period the story of the Abbey is largely

synonymous with the story of Bath itself. In a city of about 1,000 inhabitants the Priory and its satellite estates dominated the economy, and must have constituted the major employer and land owner; the other source of the city's income was

The door to the Prior's Lodging at the west end of the Abbey. In 1539 the Priory was dissolved, closing the door on eight centuries of monastic presence in Bath.

the wool trade. It is perhaps a significant indication of the level of the monastery's spirituality at this time that in 1328 the Priory's chief cook was taking home the city's third largest salary.

During the following century the tiny group of monks was clearly quite unable to maintain the great architectural legacy they had inherited. Things must have become very bad indeed by the time a new bishop, Oliver King, arrived from Wells in 1499 to make his Visitation and to assess the situation. Only an appalling state of deterioration of the building and demoralisation of the community could have led him to the radical decision he now took – to pull the church down and to start all over again. For that is what he now ordered.

4 The Storm Before The Calm

When Bishop Oliver King conducted his Visitation of the Priory in 1499 he found, as we have seen, a situation which he believed could be remedied only by the destruction of the church and its replacement by a new building. Part of the blame for this state of affairs must have lain with the negligence of the monks, whom the Bishop found to be lax, idle and greedy. Women too had been spotted inside the monastic enclosure. The Prior in charge, Prior Cantlow, was clearly too old for the post, and indeed died a month after the Visitation, his demise no doubt hastened by the shock of it all. Fifteen years earlier he had written that the Priory was "in great poverty for many causes, including the soden ruyn of the most of the church of the said Priorye and the charges and costs of repare". We may question whether the ruin was all that sudden, or whether it was due to years of neglect and mismanagement. The Bishop decided to let the monks' punishment fit their crimes: he annexed nearly three-quarters of the Priory's income for the building fund for the new Abbey. In 1500 the work commenced.

The Bishop availed himself of the Perpendicular style for the new church. This most developed form of Gothic architecture solved the structural problems of holding up the roof by the construction of external buttresses, thus making possible much larger window space, and a lighter and altogether more elegant style. Fan vaulting, a distinctively English innovation, gave a lofty and uplifting appearance to the interior. As it happened, he had actually witnessed during his education the building of two of the greatest churches constructed in this style – Eton College Chapel and the Chapel of Kings' College, Cambridge. Later he was to become a Canon of Windsor where he observed work in progress on a third – St George's Chapel. With these models in mind the Bishop set to work to build the new Priory – no longer to have Cathedral pretensions but to be just a monastic church. In his fundraising he was much aided by a dream, in which he saw angels moving up and down a ladder between heaven and earth (suspiciously similar to Jacob's vision, but dreams have no copyright: no one, in any case, has yet explained why angels, equipped with a perfectly good pair of wings, should need a ladder at all).

In the Bishop's dream a voice said "let an Olive establish the Crown and let a King restore the Church" – a clear reference to his support for his royal patron, King Henry VII, and to his divine commission to build the new church. The resulting visual pun is to be seen on either side of the West Front, flanking the angels (not all of them sure-footed) on their celestial stairway. Oliver King had set his seal upon the church he was building even if

Bishop Oliver King sets his signature on the masterpiece he planned – the new monastic church begun in 1499.

Daniel Defoe was later to condemn his West Front as "almost blasphemously decorated ... the work of superstition".

Supervised by the new and energetic Prior Birde, the work went ahead well. The Bishop's influence with Henry VII was such that the King's master masons, or architects, Robert and William Vertue, were seconded to design the new building. Of the choir fan-vaulting they promised the Bishop that "there shall be no one so goodley, neither in England nor in France". Judge for yourself if they were right.

Sadly, the Bishop died in 1503, but the work went on, although the future must have looked uncertain: the storm clouds of the Reformation were already gathering. One bizarre event was to precede it. The last Bishop of Bath and Wells before the Reformation was a non-resident Italian, Cardinal di Castello. His red Cardinal's hat is to be seen in the ceiling above the choir stalls, presiding over the Protestant worship below. On his return to Rome the

Cardinal became embroiled in a plot to murder the Pope, Leo X: the plot was uncovered and its ring leader was eliminated unpleasantly, with the aid of red hot irons. The Cardinal himself managed to escape and ended his days in what is now Turkey.

In 1996 the Abbey was honoured with a visit from the present Pope's 'Foreign Secretary', Archbishop Tauron. I was able to assure him that only two attacks on the Papacy were linked with Bath Abbey – that of the misguided Cardinal and another perpetrated by a present member of the congregation who served in the R.A.F. as a bomber pilot during the war. In a mission over Italy his navigation went astray and a bomb was released which fell into the Vatican gardens. The resulting international furore may be imagined. The Archbishop was relieved by my assurance that the whole incident was entirely accidental.

To return to the Reformation: Henry VIII's commissioners arrived to close down the Priory and to seize its assets. The usual charges were levelled about the monks' laxity, but these are un-likely to have been true after Prior Birde's effective period of office, up to his death in 1525. His Chantry Chapel, adorned with many cunning references to birds in its sculptured detail, is today in daily use for private prayer. Birde had been succeeded by Prior Holloway (also known as Gibbs). Holloway had to face the pressure now being put upon him to surrender the Priory to the King's rapacity. Even the commissioners were forced to concede Holloway's integrity, although they vilified the members of his community. Down at Glastonbury terrible things occurred later in the year when Abbot Whiting, on refusing to surrender the Abbey, was hanged, drawn and quartered. His remains are buried on the Tor, where a mound stands to this day as a monument to human wickedness and bigotry.

Whiting's terrible death lay still in the future when in Bath Holloway meekly surrendered the Priory two days before the Patronal Festival in 1539. He was allowed to spend the rest of his days pensioned off on a comfortable £80 a year. The doorway in the Abbey to the Prior's Lodging is still to be seen in the south-west corner, set up high in the wall, opening now only onto a cavity within the wall – a poignant reminder of some eight centuries of monastic life now ended. Holloway himself turned to the dubious pursuits of alchemy and the quest to discover the Philosophers' Stone, and ended his days in pathetic eccentricity.

The closure of the monastery marked a major turning point in Bath's affairs. Henceforth authority in the city would no longer revolve round Bishop and Prior, but around Mayor and Corporation. They would carry the city forward from dependence on the wool trade and agriculture to the bright prospects offered by the Baths, already being visited by a flow of gentry. The Baths were wrested from Church ownership by the Corporation, and from now on were to be developed as an economic asset.

At the time of the surrender in 1539 the great Abbey Church was far from finished. Much of the nave roof gaped open to the sky, and the south transept lacked its end wall. In 1542, Henry VIII granted the monastery "with all its houses, buildings, gardens, orchards, barns, dovecots, stables, pools, warrens, fishponds etc. within the site and precincts, together with various messages, lands, tenements (including the Prior's Park in Lyncombe, Widcombe, Holloway and Walcot, to Humfrey Colles, gent., and his heirs and assigns forever". Colles, however, almost immediately sold it on to Matthew Colthurst, who set about a vigorous asset-stripping operation. When the vultures departed, Matthew's heir, Edmund, made the city a present of "the carcass of St Peter's Church". It is good to be able to record that, despite these 16th-century atrocities, the Abbey was recently in pastoral contact with a present-day descendant of the Colthurst family. Bath's only gain from this melancholy business was the eventual establishment of its Grammar School, founded, as its name indicates, by King Edward VI with funds accrued from the dissolution of the monastery.

For much of the 16th century the Abbey lay in the city centre, unloved and unfinished, with no-one willing to undertake its completion. It was left to no less a person than Queen Elizabeth I to begin to remedy this sorry situation. In 1574 she visited Bath and was disgusted by what she saw. At that time the city's finest street was Cheap Street: it was 6' wide and had an open drain down the middle. When the Queen saw the state of the city and the ruins of the church, she was more than "not amused"; she was downright furious. At the request of the Corporation she initiated a nationwide appeal to raise funds for the church's completion.

Thomas Bellot, Steward of the House to the Queen, and Lord Burleigh, whom he served as secretary, were both active in carrying the appeal forward. A contemporary commented "the church lies still like the poore traveller ... spoiled and wounded by thieves. The Priest goes by, the Levites go by but do nothing: only a good Samaritan, honest Mr Billet, hath powr'd some oyle in the wounds and maintained it in life".

It was left to James Montagu (Bishop of Bath & Wells from 1608 to 1615) to complete the work. The story is well known of how the Bishop, on a visit to Bath, was taken round the city by a prominent citizen, Sir John Harington, a godson of Queen Elizabeth. It was raining, and the pair sought shelter in the ruins of the Abbey but found no protection in the roofless nave. "Sire," said the astute Sir John, "if the church does not keep us safe from the water above, how shall it save others from the fire below?" The Bishop took the hint and donated £1,000 to roof the nave, while his brother, a judge, later gave the ornate and splendid West Doors which still open today upon the Abbey Churchyard. The Bishop's effigy lies in state in the nave, gazing up at the roof which had been his gift.

Other local figures had been equally generous, the most remarkable being Peter Chapman. Born in 1506, he campaigned under Henry VIII at Calais and Boulogne, and then under Edward VI, Queen Mary and Queen Elizabeth I. At the age of 87 he led 800 veterans to Tilbury to help repel the Armada. He died eventually, at the age of 96, within a year of the death of Queen Elizabeth, and was buried in February 1602, having lived through six reigns. This grand old man not only paid for the completion of the North Aisle, which bears his name, but also restored St John's Hospital, the city's finest Alms House. Twenty of his descendants were to become Mayors of Bath. A contemporary Chapman in New Zealand, together with the Abbey Friends, have placed a replica of his memorial in the Chapman Aisle: the wooden original was unwisely left in the vergers' vestry in about 1800 and was no more seen, although the text survives.

In the early years of the 17th century, the Abbey Church was restored and completed, ready for its new role as a parish church which commenced in 1616. Yet it and the city had to face a fresh and bitter ordeal – that of civil war. Dr John Wroughton, in his work *A Community at War*, characterises the Civil War in Somerset as a war of religion. The Puritan/Parliamentarian element dominated Bath, while the High Anglican Royalists held Wells. Yet Bath itself was not politically monochrome. It is to the great credit of the City Council, themselves divided, that somehow they managed to hold the City together throughout these divisive times.

The war came very close to Bath in 1643 when an inconclusive battle was fought on Lansdown Hill. In it a Royalist general, Sir Bevil Grenville, was killed: a monument on the battlefield commemorates his death. Sir William Waller, the Parliament commander, retained control of Bath after the battle, though subsequent events compelled him to withdraw to Bristol and allow Royalist troops to occupy the city.

Sir William Waller had been a pre-war army friend of the Royalist commander, Sir Ralph Hopton. Waller's eve-of-battle letter to him survives, its poignancy undiminished by time: "the great God, who is the searcher of my heart, knows with what a sad sence I goe upon this service, and with what a perfect hatred I detest this warr without an Enemie ... I shall never relinquish the dear title of Your most affectionate friend". An effigy of Waller is to be seen today in the Abbey's South Aisle, where his wife is buried. His face is marred and his sword hand is hacked off, where it was the subject of a vengeful attack by Royalist soldiers quartered in Bath between 1643 and 1645. Pepys, visiting the Abbey in 1668, suffered from "a vain, pragmatical fellow who preached a ridiculous, affected sermon that made me angry". Returning the next day he noticed the carving of "a lady of Sir W. Waller's, he lying with his face broken".

The effigy of Sir William Waller, "with his face broken", in the Abbey's South Transept.

Waller's letter is now kept in the library of Prideaux Place in Padstow, Cornwall. I tracked it down in order to secure its loan and was delighted to discover that the owners, the Prideaux family, have been in possession of the house since Civil War times, when they espoused the Parliamentary cause. This *faux pas* was erased by a tactful marriage when peace returned, and the present head of the family treasures a magnificent Royal Pardon granted by King Charles II: he feels that in these days it might still serve to exonerate him should he park on a double yellow line.

With great generosity we were permitted to borrow the letter for display in the Vaults and at an unusual occasion held in Bath to mark the 300th anniversary of the Battle of Lansdown – a Civil War dinner held in Abbey Church House. We were invited to attend in 17th-century garband I was delighted to discover that my cassock would serve without alteration. I was less delighted to find out, when stew was served, that forks had not been invented at the time of the Civil War.

The Abbey served both as a barracks and, after the battle, as a hospital. At some point a godly soldier carved on the nave wall the *tetragrammaton*, the four letters of the Hebrew title for God – YHWH. Others, less godly, are thought to, have been responsible for hacking off the mitre which may once have

Puritan piety carved the Hebrew character for YHWH on the Abbey wall: perhaps done by a Parliament soldier when the Abbey was used as a hospital?

adorned the West Front statue of St Peter: the soldiers approved of Peter but hated bishops. Their animosity was similarly vented on a number of in-offensive angels, who lost their heads.

With the close of the Civil War in 1646, both religious and constitutional issues were laid to rest, at least for a time. Bath could look forward to a period of peace and consolidation to pre-pare it for the great changes which were to come during the following century.

Parliamentary counter-vandalism? Does St Peter's head grow out of his shoulders because his mitre has been hacked off?

5 Bath Booms

Bath was less heavily scarred by the Civil War than the rest of the country. Its predominantly Parliamentary sympathies (a 2:1 majority on the City Council) may have helped to leave it less divided than some communities, and pointed to the Puritan revolution that had already been taking place over the previous eight decades.

Church and City Council were closely allied in this. The City owned the right to appoint the Abbey's Rector, and in 1620 actually endowed, from the rates, a weekly biblical exposition in the Abbey on a Wednesday evening, as well as sponsoring Sunday sermons. The Rector was in charge not only of the Abbey but also of the City's other two parishes – St Michael's and St James'. All citizens had by law to attend church each Sunday. The Puritan City Fathers laboured to create a godly city, a "city set on a hill" – a mini-Geneva, no less. A policy of zero tolerance was implemented for a wide range of misdemeanours, and the proximity of the river facilitated the frequent use of the ducking stool. The scandal of mixed bathing in the hot baths was removed by a rigid rule of segregation (exactly mirroring a similar enactment passed by the Emperor Hadrian 17 centuries before; people never learn).

Because of the city's Puritan complexion, reflected in the Abbey's congregation, the Abbey did not become a target for attack as other large churches and cathedrals did (apart from the military vandalism already noted): it was seen as "our church", and left otherwise unmolested. When Queen Elizabeth I had launched her national appeal for funds, the City Council had stated that covered space was needed "to hear sermons". In other words the completed Abbey was intended to be a Puritan preaching centre. There must have been many members of the Abbey congregation in Colonel Popham's Bath Regiment of Trained Bands which sacked Wells Cathedral and the Bishop's Palace in 1642. Wells meant the Bishop, and the Bishop meant the King and Archbishop Laud, whose attempts to restore a more catholic order in the churches had proved so provocative and, for Laud himself, fatal, provoking his trial and execution.

In Bath the City Council sought to ensure a Puritan tone in the Abbey's worship, although the new Rector whom they appointed in 1639 had clearly bamboozled them. To their horror he turned out to have Royalist sympathies. In 1645 he was accordingly dismissed and two safe Puritans appointed in his stead. They had, however, reckoned without the Rector's wife who shut herself up in the Rectory and barred the door to them. After a time the siege was lifted and the disconsolate Puritans disappeared from the scene. No further appointment was made for three years.

After the Restoration of the Monarchy in 1660, peace and reconciliation gradually returned to Bath and to its Abbey. The Prayer Book, albeit revised with some dangerous innovations, replaced the Presbyterian Directory of Worship which had formed the congregation's meagre fare during the Commonwealth. Demand for the Prayer Book actually provoked street demonstrations and aroused passions perfectly intelligible to today's Abbey congregation. It became once again permissible to celebrate Easter, Whitsunday, Christmas and Saints' Days – all of which commemorations had actually been made illegal after the Civil War. No longer was it necessary to undergo a searching examination and receive a ticket before you could be admitted to Holy Communion. Of all the Puritan reforms, only the rule imposing two sermons per Sunday survived; nowadays they have been increased to four.

Even before the Restoration, the Independent element which predominated in Cromwell's army had begun to prevail over the rigidities of Presbyterianism. Independents believed in the right of each congregation to go its own way and such a belief led to a more tolerant attitude generally towards different forms of religious expression. This trend was accelerated by the intro-duction of balanced forms of Anglicanism. In Bath the result was the exodus of the more extreme Puritans from the Abbey to form their own congregations.

Extremism from the opposite direction impinged sensationally on the Abbey's life in 1687 when King James II – a declared Roman Catholic – visited the church. With him came his chaplain, Father John Huddleston (from a clerical family still notable in our own day): first he celebrated the Eucharist in a thoroughly Catholic fashion, and then he actually preached a sermon advocating return to Rome. Yet more alarm was caused when the King himself followed ancient custom by "touching for the King's evil" – laying hands for healing on those with scrofulous skin diseases. Not only was this deemed superstitious but it also lent support to the doctrine of the Divine Right of Kings: had there not just been a civil war to eradicate that very doctrine? Next morning the saintly Bishop Ken, who had been outraged by these unheralded goings-on, held a service of cleansing in the Abbey to exorcise such deplorable happenings.

Nevertheless, it was ironic that the King's action pointed prophetically forward to Bath's major role in the next century as a centre for health tourism. On the same occasion of the King's visit, his Queen, Mary of Modena, bathed in the waters, seeking a cure for her apparent infertility. Within a year she was pregnant and the resultant publicity did the Baths' commercial appeal no harm at all. The son born to her, however, was to become "the Old Pretender", and Bath's links with him were to prove a source of trouble in the future. This royal endorsement of the Baths was further strengthened by the visits of Queen Anne in 1702 and 1703. Bath's future was now assured, and the great and the good began to pour in annually to benefit from the city's allegedly therapeutic waters.

Bath's ensuing meteoric growth in the first half of the 18th century was due in large part to that remarkable triumvirate – Beau Nash, appointed by the City Council as Master of Ceremonies in 1708 (and later to earn for himself his own informal title of 'King of Bath'); Ralph Allen, the entrepreneur, who profitably revolutionised our postal service, invested in the Avon Canal Project, and opened up the mines on the south side of Bath; and John Wood, the architect, who adapted classical styles to Bath's hills and combes, and who was to be followed in this task by his son of the same name. It was Bath's good fortune to have such a trio of stars in conjunction. For 50 years Nash built up Bath's reputation as the place you had to visit if you were any one at all. John Wood transformed a modest country town into a metropolitan spa adorned with the most elegant architecture, in a homogeneity not found in other English cities. Ralph Allen made it all possible by excavating the Bath stone in Combe Down and whizzing it down the hill by an ingenious zig-zagging railway which he constructed in what is now Ralph Allen Drive.

Bath's 18th-century building boom burst out of the city's medieval walls, built over the Roman fortifications. Only reconstructed frag-ments remain (above).

Bath's sole remaining city gate (left) – *the Eastgate, hidden from view behind the Empire Hotel.*

His career may well have advanced by his role in uncovering a Jacobite plot to stage an armed uprising in sympathy with the Old Pretender's 1715 rebellion. Even the Abbey Rector's name was linked with this dastardly plan. There was much local feeling for the Prince who was for Bath in a special sense "our boy". As H-hour drew near, many well-known Jacobites began to converge on the city. The loyalist wife of the Bishop of Durham, who happened to be staying in Bath, was particularly incensed when the Abbey's ringers rang rapturously to welcome one of them, Sir William Wyndham. She took issue with the seditious bellmen, demanding that they ring also for the first anniversary of George I's arrival in England. They demurred, pleading that it might give offence to the "mixed company" gathered in the city: she nevertheless compelled them to comply by threatening to disclose their disloyal refusal.

The Government, by now thoroughly alarmed, occupied the city with a force of cavalry. Someone – possibly Ralph Allen – revealed the existence of an arms cache sufficient to equip 200 men, with carbines, swords and even three cannon. The game was up and the city's chastened magistrates and Council swore undying loyalty to the House of Hanover. The force which occupied the city was commanded by Major-General Wade, later to become the city's MP in 1722 and the Abbey's Churchwarden.

In the latter capacity he commissioned a magnificent altarpiece of The Wise Men bearing gifts to the infant Christ; the painting may now be the work depicting that theme among the Prior Park Collection. One of The Wise Men bears a close resemblance to the good General, later a Field Marshal. So great was the fame – or notoriety – he had acquired as a result of his part in the 'pacification' of the Scottish Highlands that an extra verse for the National Anthem was composed in his honour. It celebrates his part in the ethnic cleansing in terms that would make Slobodan Milosevic blush.

With these excitements behind them, Bathonians settled down to the serious business of pleasure-seeking, money-making and building. Under Nash's benevolent autocracy a regimen was developed which included prayers at the Abbey, breakfast in the Pump Room, promenades on Grand Parade, the consumption of appalling quantities of the malodorous water and compulsory attendance at the nightly balls. High society loved it and Nash made it even more attractively secure by getting the City Council to ban the wearing of swords inside the city. Not all comment, however, was favourable. Even allowing for satire, this anonymous 1730's poem no doubt contains some truth:

> What sickly, crude, offensive vapours there
> The nostrils snuff up with the tainted Air!
> Whole groups of Foppish Slovens fouly fine
> In dirty Shirts, and Tinsel stink and shine;
> Midst crowds of Dames, who in their nightly Trim
> Just reeking from their Bed, still stew and steam.

Later in the century, a Cornish clergyman, the Revd John Penrose wrote sourly in 1767: "The Bath ladies are not very lovely. The very fashions, which fine ladies must follow, or they had as good be out of the world, will not even suffer them to be wholesome. Such ladies as have their own hair, not artificial, and have it dressed by the barber, do not comb their heads for three months together. Whether they kill the lice with quicksilver or a hammer is a secret."

Others however could view the social scene with a less jaundiced eye. Sophie Carey, in the 1720s writes: "there are public breakfasts later in the morning, sometimes with music or lectures on art and hot chocolate and Sally Lunn cakes with butter which, Aunt Ursula swears, undo all the good of the baths. She nibbles instead the new biscuits invented by Dr Oliver". Anstey's 1766 *New Guide to Bath* sums it all up as follows:

> Paid bells and musicians,
> Drugs, nurse and physicians,
> Balls, raffles, subscriptions and chairs:
> Wigs, gowns, skins and trimming,
> Good books for the women,
> Plays, concerts, tea, cordial and prayers

Bath's star was in the ascendant throughout the 18th century, and the city's development continued apace to keep up with it all. John Wood the Elder aped the Colosseum in building the Circus, while his son broke new ground by constructing the Royal Crescent to fit snugly into the indented slopes of Lansdown Hill.

However, all good things have their day. Bath's decline was due to two factors – the vagaries of fashion and the outbreak of war with France. It was royal patronage that had triggered Bath's expansion; and it was royal whim which led high society elsewhere. No reigning Hanoverian had visited Bath to polish up the cachet bestowed by Queen Anne. And then, quite simply, George Ill discovered the seaside. First Weymouth and then Brighton, under George IV's patronage, punctured Bath's bubble.

A much graver setback, however, resulted from the French Revolution and the ensuing war which broke out in 1793. The elaborate fabric of credit which supported Bath's building boom collapsed like a pack of cards. Bankruptcies proliferated in the building trade. At the same time serious poverty amongst Bath's unemployed caused anxieties within a society that was already

Field-Marshal Wade's elegant residence stands next to the Abbey where he was churchwarden.

An Englishman's castle: was Sham Castle purely Ralph Allen's experiment in using Bath stone or was it a piece of triumphant self-assertion?

For actually living in, Ralph Allen built Prior Park –

– and as a pied à terre, *in the city centre, he built this town house.*

looking apprehensively over its shoulder at events on the other side of the Channel. A proliferation of charities sprang up – some 14 between 1790 and 1811 – motivated no doubt by genuine concern but also by anxieties about civil unrest. The most significant of the genuine charities survives to this day – the Monmouth Street Society. By the turn of the century a third of the population – some 10,000 people – were receiving a weekly rice ration. Note, by the way, the meteoric rise in that population: it had increased tenfold from 3,000 in 1700 to some 30,000 by 1800.

The first stages of Baths's decline are perhaps reflected in Jane Austen's two novels with a Bath setting – *Northanger Abbey* and *Persuasion*. The former was written shortly after Jane's own first visit to Bath in 1797, at the age of 21. We may expect its central character, the young Catherine Morland, to reflect something of Jane's own reactions to the city: "I really believe I shall always be talking of Bath – I do like it so very much. Oh, who can ever be tired of Bath?" Yet the later book, written in 1816, ten years after Jane left Bath, contains this jaded comment on the petty snobbery to which Bath society was descending: "All that remained was to marshal themselves and to proceed into the concert room and to be of all the consequence in their power, draw as many eyes, excite as many whispers, and disturb as many people as they could".

Meanwhile, what was happening at the Abbey? What impact did it have on the city's spiritual life when Bath became such a mecca for secular pilgrimage? It is to this enquiry that we must now turn.

6 The Age of Reason

We have seen how Bath's explosive renaissance in the 18th century received its kick-start from the scandalous events in the Abbey during the visit of King James II in 1687 and his Queen's subsequent and fruitful visit to the Baths. Once again the spirit of the goddess Sulis-Minerva, in her benign role as Healer, seemed to hover over the steaming waters. The marvel of hot water bubbling up mysteriously from underground exerted its numinous fascination, even upon people poised to move forward into the Brave New World of the Age of Reason.

It was in 1628 that the French mathematician René Descartes had sought intellectual freedom in Holland to apply himself to the business of seeking certainty. This he did by setting systematic doubt against every possible proposition he could imagine, so as to see if, at the end of the process, he was going to be left with any indubitable foundation on which true knowledge could be built up. Famously he was reduced to but one statement which he was unable to doubt: "I think, therefore I am".

It is no exaggeration to say that the whole scientific revolution of the last three centuries and much of the mind set of contemporary society stems from Descartes' principle of systematic doubt. From now on the only sort of certainty which could be accepted was the certainty that springs from hard, indubitable evidence open to empirical verification. Such have been the practical benefits of this liberating revolution that it has taken people 300 years to realise its limitations. However valuable such an approach might be in the laboratory, it is limiting and oppressive when applied to the world of values and human relationships. Whoever proposed marriage on the basis of a series of scientific experiments carried out upon his hapless and unsuspecting fiancée? Can anyone prove scientifically that Beethoven was a genius, that stealing is wrong, or that God is love?

The knock-on effect of this new thinking – the Enlightenment, as it came to be called – on the world of religion was at first unsettling, if ultimately salutary. The Bible was soon to be stretched upon the rack of scientific enquiry; all beliefs and traditions could now be radically questioned, and were. The final

A 1788 print depicts Abbey worship – perhaps a no-doubt compulsory Bluecoat School service. Those who find the Abbey pews hard should note the total absence of nave seating. (Print by Samuel Hieronymus Grimm, MS15546.f.101, reproduced by permission of The British Library)

confrontation between religion and the new scientific thinking was not to come until the 19th century, with the celebrated controversy between Darwin and Bishop Wilberforce over the Theory of Evolution: the seeds of the conflict, however, were already evident in the 18th century.

While the intellectual giants battled it out overhead, the parish clergy kept their heads down and got on with their job as best they could. Yet they could not help but be infected by a certain theological malaise. The only respectable role for God to occupy, it seemed, was as a sort of rational principle in a world where everything was achieved by reason and order. The moral teaching of Christianity was seen as the reasonable conclusion that would be arrived at by any sensible person. Intellectual enquiry was in: revelation was out.

Such a theological starting point led to a dutiful, conventional, and thoroughly tedious form of religion. Prayer, spirituality and sacrificial commitment were at a low ebb throughout much of the life of the Established Church in the first half of the 18th century. The diaries of Parson Woodforde, for example, leave one in no doubt of that. On one Christmas Day he does not manage to get to church, but records his dinner menu in meticulous detail.

The tepid conformity of the time would no doubt have characterised Bath Abbey in the early years of the 18th century. The City Council, as we have seen, appointed the Abbey's Rector, and they were certainly going to make sure he would not be someone to rock the boat and scare away the society folk flocking to Bath each year in such encouraging numbers. Prayers at the Abbey were an important part of the regime. No one must be allowed to scare off the customers with an unseemly display of religious 'enthusiasm' – the ultimate insult in church circles at that time.

Even the classical architecture, extending ever more widely across a city that at times resembled one big building site, reinforced the message. It was ordered and rational and, for the most part, safely horizontal. Few spires were permitted to point people to heaven or form a lightning conductor for the love of God. Classical Bath spoke to people of the human wisdom that originated ultimately from Athens, not the divine revelation that flashed down to earth at Jerusalem. So sure of itself was this new Age of Reason that its sense of superiority over preceding centuries extended even to architecture. The word 'gothic' in this context was originally a term of abuse. It smacked of the dark ages of myth and superstition. No wonder John Wood likened the angels

The Pump Room, completed in 1796, exhibits the Age of Reason set in stone.

A sedan chair as seen by John Penrose in the Abbey in 1766.

on the Abbey's West Front to so many bats clinging to the stonework. When such scorn was poured onto church buildings, the faith itself also had to suffer in public esteem. Clergy morale was bound to be affected.

Two mid-century observations support the picture of a tepid theology producing a slothful religion. The Revd John Penrose, up from Cornwall, observed in 1766: "last Sunday at church a lady was brought in a sedan and placed before the reading desk in the Abbey and remained in it all service time. And this morning, another lady the same: and after prayers was carried to the Communion Table to be churched, and did not come out of the sedan at all!" In the same year Tobias Smollett wrote yet more unkindly: "there is always a great show of the clergy at Bath; none of your thin, puny, yellow, hectic figures, exhausted with abstinence and hard study but great overgrown dignitaries and rectors, with rubicund noses and gouty ankles, or broad bloated faces, dragging along great swag bellies: the emblems of sloth and indigestion".

If a superficial theology and formalised worship produced meagre spiritual nourishment at the Abbey throughout much of the 18th century, there was another yet more distasteful factor that served as a dissuasive to would-be Abbey churchgoers. We should like to draw a veil over this matter, but the demands of honesty force us to mention it.

In a word, the Abbey stank. The nave was used frequently for burials up to 1845. When need arose, a floor slab or two were

The Abbey's memorials testify to "the vast number of bodies buried within the church", and to the ineffectiveness of Bath water in curing people.

lifted and a new walled grave prepared. *The New Prose Bath Guide* for 1778 has this to say: "it is very doubtful whether the Abbey Church is not, on many accounts, a very improper place (except to people in Full Health) to attend Divine Service. The vast number of bodies buried within the church and near the surface and the Frequency of the Ground being opened, before the effect of Putrefaction is over, the Doors and Windows not being sufficiently or constantly kept open, renders the confined Air perceptibly disagreeable on first entering the church and, we are told, there is an Opening or Ventilator in the Roof, over which if any one placed their Nose, they will meet at all times a Stench scarce to be imagined ... The malignant sore Throat is not very uncommon at Bath, and who can say from what source of corruption it arises?"

A macabre reminder of the Abbey's past function turned up in the course of the Heritage Vaults excavations – a collection of 16th-century coffin-handles, no doubt stock-in-trade of some itinerant purveyor of fine coffins to the gentry.

Not only did the Abbey smell; it was also cold, and a comfort-loving age would not put up with it. It is not, therefore, very surprising that a rash of alternative conventicles sprang up in

Bath during the 18th century and proved immediately popular. These were the 'proprietary chapels', chapels within the Church of England but run by groups of subscribers who had licence to appoint their own minister, and to order the building as they wished (the Octagon Chapel had six large stoves). The proprietors even received a dividend from the pew rents paid. You could thus come to a church where you could enjoy perfect comfort and hear exactly the sort of sermon that you wanted to hear, without being disturbed in any way at all. Such establishments pandered perfectly to the worst aspects of Bath society. There was one exception to this generality of the bland leading the bland, and that was the Countess of Huntingdon's Chapel in the Paragon, of which more anon.

Into this complacent pond a stone was cast which was to cause many ripples both within Bath and far beyond. The stone was called John Wesley. He first visited the city in April 1739 and was to return fully 100 times more over the next 51 years, preaching on some 150 occasions. We must turn now to examine just why he was so significant for this city which he called "Satan's Throne".

Bath's joie de vivre breaks out in its buskers.
Some may feel, though, that this is the best type of act – the silent variety.

49

The incomparable Royal Crescent.

Bath in bloom: Victoria Park at its best.

Bath's Lanes are a delightful contrast to our grander boulevards.

The Abbey's West Front tells its story to tourists and residents alike.

Not an ecclesiastical fashion parade, but a meeting with our opposite numbers from Braunschweig's Lutheran Cathedral.

The Abbey congregation re-enact Palm Sunday.
(Photo by kind permission of Fotek)

*Laurence Tindall's fine sculpture of the Risen Lord
taking shape outside the Abbey.*

7 Satan's Throne

It was in May 1738 that the Revd John Wesley had found his heart "strangely warmed" in the course of listening to a Bible Study on St Paul's Letter to the Romans, at the Moravian Chapel in London. It was a moment to be compared with Paul's own experience on the Damascus Road, and the consequences were also to be global.

A year later, in a Bristol brickyard, he embarked on his career as an open-air preacher, and in the same month he visited Bath for the first time. Only London, Bristol and Kingswood were to see more of him during his itinerant ministry over the next half century, in which he was to cover some quarter of a million miles on horseback. Yet, as already mentioned, his name for the city was "Satan's Throne", and his brother Charles referred to Bath as "that Sodom of our land". The Bath to which Wesley came was still a little city nestling for the most part within its medieval walls. His impact must have been city-wide.

What was new about his message? What was he saying that could not be heard on Sunday in the parish churches? Just as with St Paul, the rest of Wesley's life was to be the working out of his own conversion. He had discovered that the Christian Gospel demands a personal and individual response to the Cross of Christ, which would involve an admission of one's own sinfulness; through this response came the liberating experience of receiving God's grace, freely given but impossible to earn. This grace was a real force to transform life. Wesley believed that this was the most important discovery a person could make. It would therefore necessarily demand the dedication of the rest of a person's life to communicate the open secret of God's love. That was the Evangelical emphasis. That was what drove Wesley.

This message, which only echoed the discovery of St Paul and Martin Luther to name but two, came as dynamite detonated under the thin crust of theology and dutifulness displayed by the Established Church. It made Wesley very unpopular with his fellow clergy. Called to account by Bishop Butler, he received the stinging rebuke – "Sir, this pretending to extraordinary revelations and gifts of the Holy Ghost is a horrid thing – a very horrid thing".

The sole equestrian statue of John Wesley, in the forecourt of the New Room, Bristol. (Photo by courtesy of the Redcliffe Press Ltd, Bristol)

Despite the Bishop, Wesley's message proved immensely popular, especially among the unchurched thousands of working people. In Bath his problem was always to find a field large enough to contain the numbers who flocked to hear him preach. Inevitably he was pilloried by Bath's aristocratic visitors who disliked being told that they were "under sin", and he was ostracised by his fellow clergy, who resented the theft of many in their congregations. His particular *bête noire*, predictably, was Beau Nash, who opposed him at every turn. If Bath was Satan's Throne, it was pretty clear who, for Wesley, personified Satan.

Early on Nash tried to break up an open-air meeting being addressed by Wesley, whom he threatened in the name of the King, demanding to know under what authority Wesley preached. He replied: "by the authority of Jesus Christ, conveyed to me by the Archbishop of Canterbury when he laid his hands upon me and said 'Take thou authority to preach the Gospel'". Nash pressed him:

"Your preaching frightens people out of their wits."

"Sir, did you ever hear me preach?"

"No."

"How then can you judge of what you never heard?"

"Sir, by common report."

"Common report is not enough. Is not your name Nash?"

"My name is Nash."

"Sir, I dare not judge of you by common report."

At this the baffled and infuriated Nash departed.

The story is told too of a later encounter, head-on, on the pavement in the city centre. Nash, standing his ground, snarled: "I never give way to fools and blackguards". "But I always do", answered Wesley meekly, and stepped off the pavement.

The movement of which Wesley was the forerunner was to have a big

Wesley's great opponent in Bath was the sardonic Beau Nash.

impact on Bath: indeed, it still does. It is worth enquiring into its character.

Its essential message, as we have seen, was personal, challenging people to individual commitment. Delivered in the streets and not from the pulpit, and in every day language, rather than the erudite remoteness of the conventional preaching of the day, it proved immensely appealing in an age still susceptible to mass movements. The story is told of Wesley preaching to miners coming off the night shift in Kingswood, as it was getting light. So moved were many of his hearers, that tears could be seen coursing down their cheeks, making channels through the coaldust on their faces.

Untroubled by the anxieties about manipulation that would have concerned a later age, Evangelical preachers were quite uninhibited in their use of histrionics. One of them, a man named Berridge, once sent this advice to a newly-appointed preacher: "Rip up your audience, and Moses will lend you a carving knife". As in all times of revival, the movement was characterised by a flowering of new hymns and songs – the best of them powerful, if personal ("Amazing grace ...", "When I survey ..."). Others of them were nauseatingly individualistic and pietistic ("Upwards I fly/Quite justified I").

What began as a liberation movement for people imprisoned in hidebound churches, or excluded by poverty from the Christian faith altogether, notched up many great achievements in reforming and improving every aspect of life. Yet in its later stages it ran to seed into a moralistic and restrictive teaching that was narrowing and limiting. Some even go so far as to blame Bath's numerous Evangelical clergy for the city's decline in the 1830s; the relentless salvoes from the pulpit against frivolity and extravagance were said to be frightening off the visitors.

Before assenting too quickly to this stereotypical view, it is worth recollecting the massive reforms in our national life which came about through the efforts of three Bathonians of influence and evangelical conviction.

The Countess of Huntingdon has already been mentioned. Just to look at a portrait of her is to be made aware immediately of her formidable and determined character. At the chapel she had built in The Paragon (now The Building of Bath Museum) she reigned supreme. One visiting preacher who had suffered her dictatorial ways is on record as having departed muttering: "My instructions must come from the Lamb, not from the Lamb's wife". Her contribution was to carry the Evangelical message to the aristocratic circles in Bath society, and so to disseminate that reformation in public standards that marked the end of the 18th century. King George III is on record as having declared that he "wished to God there was a Lady Huntingdon in every diocese of the kingdom".

Hannah More, who lived in Great Pulteney Street for 10 years from 1792, appeared less formidable than the Countess, but actually achieved even greater results. She and her four sisters were much moved by the plight of children in the poor mining communities of the Mendips who had no opportunity to learn to read and write, let alone to study the Bible. She deployed her considerable resources with great generosity to do something about it. The main thrust of her efforts was to spread the faith in areas largely abandoned by the Church: in 13 communities in the Mendips at that time there was not one resident cleric. She built up a network of Sunday Schools and day schools, and published cheap tracts for the poor to read: they bought 2 million of these tracts in the first year of publication. The poet Southey's appreciation of her is perceptive: "Her manners are mild, her information considerable, and her taste correct. There are five sisters, and each of them would be remarked in a mixed company; they pay for, and direct, the education of 1000 poor children." The long-term effect of Hannah's work was to encourage the growth of Church day schools across the country. These in their turn were the bedrock on which our state education system was then to be built up.

The greatest of our trio of Evangelicals was a Pulteney Street friend and neighbour of Hannah More – William Wilberforce. Charming but indolent as a young man, he wrote of his time at St John's College, Cambridge, in 1776: "I supped with my tutor, and was introduced to two of the most gambling vicious characters perhaps in all England ... My tutor never urged me to attend lectures – and I never did".

However, the deficiencies of a Cambridge education were remedied when another Cambridge don, the Revd Isaac Milner, accompanied Wilberforce and his mother on a continental holiday in 1784. Through long and earnest conversations in the course of their travels, the young MP for Hull – for that is what Wilberforce had become – came to a profound commitment of his life to Christ. Encouraged to remain in public life, he confided later in his diary: "God Almighty has set before me two great objects – the reformation of manners and the suppression of the slave trade".

A man of poor physique and fragile health, his labours and achievements were heroic. Humanizing life in prison, ending bull-bating, educating the poor and the deaf – these were just some of his concerns; at one time he was actively engaged in directing no less than 69 charities. His great concern – to raise public standards by converting the leading members of society – was promoted through the Proclamation Society, which enlisted the top people actually to live out and to promote the monarch's traditional assertion of moral standards, made on acceding to the throne; and through the publication of his magnum opus – *A Practical View of the Prevailing Religious System of Professed Christians in the Upper and Middle Classes of the Country, contrasted with Real Christianity*. Wooed no doubt by its snappy-catch title people bought this work by the thousand and it rapidly ran through five editions.

William Wilberforce was a frequent visitor to Bath and a near-neighbour in Great Pulteney Street to his friend, Hannah More. (Print by courtesy of the National Portrait Gallery)

Important though these initiatives were, the life's work for which he is best remembered is, of course, his campaign against, first, the slave trade and, second, slavery itself. Wilberforce was the parliamentary spokesman for a growing humanitarian movement and he waged his campaign with tenacity and eventual success. News of the successful passage of his abolition bill reached him on his death bed.

If all these achievements make him sound worthy rather than attractive, we need to remember his amazing personal charisma which kept him throughout his life at the centre of a wide circle of friends. His wit and powers of mimicry were much enjoyed. Entering a Bath drawing room missionary meeting he was heard to remark: "Just like hell: you can't get near the fire for parsons". He once compared the House of Commons to Noah's Ark: "many beasts and a few humans". This lovable and attractive saint made many visits to Bath, primarily to recover his health, and in 1796 he was married in Walcot Parish Church. Hannah More, his great friend, said of him that she rejoiced that "there was one efficient statesman, who fervently prayed for every measure he was engaged in, and who committed the event to the divine superintendence".

These, then, were the Evangelicals in Bath. If some of their clergy may rightly be censured in the later stages of the movement for their killjoy and restrictive attitudes, let us hold that in balance with the fact that the Evangelical movement as a whole initiated a widespread improvement in standards of honesty and integrity in public life; that they laid the foundations for universal education; that they improved the condition of the poor in many ways; and that they brought about the eradication of the greatest moral blot on the nation's character – slavery. Not a bad record. We might even be modestly proud that so much of the Evangelical Revival was hatched right here, in Bath.

8 From Decay to Change

We left the economic life of Bath in the doldrums, due to the bankruptcies caused by the war with France, and by the exodus of the fashionable visitors who had departed in search of fresh fields and pastures new. By the end of the 18th century, the composition and economy of the city had changed. No longer was it a small country town enabled to play host to an annual immigration of high society. This immigration had been made possible by geography, architecture and the happy issuing from the earth of hot water which had fallen as rain on the Mendips 10,000 years earlier.

The distinguished visitors continued to arrive, if not in such numbers, but the resident population had now grown dramatically. The early years of the new century, it is true, were to welcome the widowed Lady Nelson to Bath, with Lady Hamilton living embarrassingly just round the corner. George Ill's Queen Charlotte resided for a time in Bath. But the flow of eminent people was to diminish. No longer were leading artists such as Gainsborough, Hoare and Lawrence able to derive such a lucrative income from painting the visitors' portraits. From now on Bath had to stand more firmly on its own two feet.

It managed to do this only with difficulty during the opening decades of the century. Along with the rest of the country, it had to face up to the abolition of the cosily incestuous oligarchy that had controlled its affairs. Constitutional reform was in the air, and although Bath was to avoid the violent rioting that erupted in Bristol, the struggle was real enough in Bath as well. Two years after the young Princess Victoria opened the park named in her honour, the Reform Act of 1832 was passed just in time to serve as a constitutional safety valve. Instead of the one Tory and one Whig MP habitually and amicably sent to Westminster by the 30 or so electors, the new electorate of 2,835 chose instead a Whig and an out-and-out Radical.

In the following year local government received a similar jolt, with the result that in the 1835 Council elections, 16 out of the 42 Councillors elected were branded by the *Bath Chronicle* as "downright radicals".

There was plenty to be radical about. Law and order was an issue demanding immediate attention. There were no less than three separate police authorities for different areas of the city, while Widcombe had none. Now a force of 144 of Bath's finest was brought into being to police the whole city.

The urgency of this reform reflected the temptation to crime posed by the scandalous disparity of wealth within the city at that time. While most Bathonians continued to exist in affluence or at least in seedy gentility, the slums round Avon Street were universally held to be sinks of poverty and iniquity, the breeding ground for crime. Tainted water supplies and occasional flooding produced public health hazards that were to last right up until 1870, when the Water Act compelled municipal meanness at last to agree to construct the Monkswood Reservoir. As late as 1865 4,000 homes lacked a water supply altogether or had to rely on a polluted source. Epidemics of smallpox and typhus were rife. Cholera claimed 90 victims in 1849. Such poverty in the midst of affluence was more scandalous in a small city where no one could plead ignorance of the state of affairs. Within a small community poverty and disease were further concentrated by area and income group. The average age of death given in an 1841 report, points up the appalling inequality:

Gentlemen and professional persons – 55 years;
Tradesmen and farmers – 37 years;
Mechanics and labourers – 25 years.

Yet reform and progress were in the air. Isambard Kingdom Brunel's railway came to Bath in 1840 and connected the city to the wider world and its new thinking.

It is good to record that a distinguished Abbey Rector, the Revd Charles Kemble, was, for seven years running, the Chairman of the Hospital Board that in 1868 brought into being the Royal United Hospital, alongside the Mineral Water Hospital (founded a century earlier by, amongst others, Dr Oliver of the eponymous biscuit and the much maligned Beau Nash).

Schools already abounded in the city; in 1854 it is recorded that three-quarters of Bath's children attended the city's 50 day schools, most of them run by the churches. Charles Kemble was also elected Chairman of the School Board, responsible for implementing the 1870 Education Act. In that capacity he oversaw the establishment of universal elementary education across Bath.

The churches continued to occupy a central position within the city's life, and the century saw a major boom in church building. The last outbreak of religious intolerance had occurred in 1780 when mobs, inflamed by the Gordon Riots in London, had rioted and actually burnt down the Roman Catholic Chapel. It is much to the credit of the authorities that the riot was put down speedily. Its ringleader, a footman, was sought out, arrested and hanged, and generous compensation was paid to the Roman Catholic community. Since that time whatever religious excitement the city had experienced had been of a more positive kind. The continuing effects of the Evangelical Revival were deeply embedded in Bath's parishes and evinced a three–dimensional concern for people's material wellbeing as well as for their spiritual salvation.

There was a particular reason why most Bath Church of England parishes shared – and still share – an Evangelical emphasis in their teaching. One of the great forefathers of the movement had been the Revd Charles Simeon, Vicar of Holy Trinity, Cambridge, for no less than 53 years – his whole ministry – from 1783 onwards. Part of the Evangelical message, as we have seen, was the challenge to personal commitment. Such an approach from the pulpit, however, becomes tedious when repeated week by week with the same congregation; you cannot keep converting the same people every Sunday (though some still try!). The solution to this problem was simple: either you or the congregation have to keep on the move. This led Evangelical clergy to 'itinerate', travelling round the country and preaching, often in the open-air, and without the permission of the parish clergy in whose pastures they were trespassing. So much resentment did this practice cause that it forced many itinerant clergy to leave the Church of England for the greater freedom of Non-Conformity.

There was, however, another solution – to deliver one's evangelising message in a place where it was the congregation who were on the move. Such situations occurred in the universities, and, to a lesser extent in spa towns like Bath, where there was an annual migration of visitors. Clergy in these settings, like Charles Simeon, were more likely to enjoy a fruitful ministry still within the Church of England. Charles Simeon himself was staunchly Anglican all his days.

Simeon, however, had a wider vision – to extend the Evangelical message to centres of influence across the land. He achieved this by setting up a charitable trust to buy up the livings of churches in the key areas that he targeted. So it was that, when a new law prevented municipal ownership of advowsons (the right to appoint a Rector or Vicar), the Simeon Trustees moved in quickly and in 1834 purchased Bath Abbey. Today, the Simeon Trustees are patrons of seven parishes in and around Bath.

At the Abbey we have sought to maintain the Simeon spirit in vastly different times. Certainly the great man would be delighted to share in the Abbey's worship on Easter morning. The 11 o'clock service – packed out for the occasion and with one of our Bishops as preacher – begins as normal within the church but concludes outside in the Abbey Churchyard. The longest Easter hymn in the book enables the congregation of some 1,200 to process out and form a great horseshoe facing the West Front. A trumpet fanfare from the West Front gallery causes the coffee-drinkers at Binks to choke in mid-cappuccino, and the visiting Bishop is then given three minutes to deliver an Easter message. When I initiated this act of celebration and proclamation in 1990, I did so with much fear and trepidation: within a couple of years it had become a part of the great Abbey tradition. Simeon would love it.

It was, then, the Simeon Trustees who did Bath and the Abbey the great service of appointing, in 1859, the Revd Charles Kemble, whose contribution to reforms in the city we have noted. Somehow he found time and energy to renew the face of the Abbey also. Evangelical clergy are traditionally scorned for being Philistines who regard the maintenance and repair of great churches as a millstone round their necks: Kemble, however, was much more positive. He saw the Abbey as a launchpad for his message and wanted it rendered a more beautiful and effective instrument for preaching the Gospel, plans facilitated by his personal wealth from which he contributed generously. His two major achievements, in collaboration with Sir George Gilbert Scott, the architect, were to complete the fan-vaulting down the nave, at that time roofed over with Bishop Montagu's barrel vaulting; and to strip out the organ screen across the Chancel which effectively cut the church in two. We may today stand in the nave and look up at Kemble's coat of arms and give thanks for all that his energy achieved in his 15 years as Rector. His death at the age of 55 in 1874 was a loss to both City and Abbey.

If Kemble's period as Rector lasted 15 years, the prize for length of ecclesiastical office in Bath must surely go to a Nonconformist, the Revd William Jay, who was Minister of Argyle Street Chapel for no less than 61 years, from 1791 to 1852. He was much respected and admired as a preacher: Sheridan delivered on him the verdict that he was – "the most manly orator he had ever heard". During his long incumbency he had seen the Napoleonic Wars through from the start; shared in Bath's resulting economic depression; observed the popular head of steam that preceded the Reform Act of 1832; wondered at a more literal head of steam when Brunel's locomotives began to chuff through Bath; and caught the mood of reform and progress that was beginning to usher in a new era of prosperity.

Bath itself was to make its own contribution to scientific progress. In 1840 a wealthy landowner living out at Lacock, Fox Talbot, had taken the world's first photograph printed from a negative – a rather dull picture of a casement at Lacock Abbey. In the city itself William Friese-Green and John Rudge were later to play midwife to cinematography by developing cine film. The two-stroke engine stuttered into life up on Combe Down. And this is to name but a few Bathonian innovations.

Brunel's railway, here seen in its Sydney Gardens cutting, reached Bath in 1841. It marked the end of Bath's relative isolation.

The second half of the 19th century was to see a renaissance in Bath. Communications improved with rail links being established both north and south of the city – the Midland Railway and the Somerset & Dorset Railway (the latter to become known affectionately as 'the Slow and Dirty'). Hotels and shops blossomed and flourished as Bath became a more desirable venue for conventions and other large gatherings. The Royal Association had met in Bath in 1864 and heard David Livingstone's impassioned speech about the iniquities of slavery in central Africa.

In 1873 the national Church Congress packed out the Abbey. The Revd Francis Kilvert confided to his diary: "This morning I went to Bath with my father and mother to attend the Church Congress service at the Abbey. Dr Alexander, the Bishop of Derry, preached an admirable sermon nearly an hour long." On the Friday following he "attended three sections of the Church Congress at the Congress Hall. The subjects were the Life of Godliness, Religious Wants and Claims of Children, and Church Music." It is a relief to discover that Francis was capable of being distracted from these high-flown themes: "In the morning as Bishop Ryan was speaking, an angel came into the Congress Hall and stood near the door listening. It had taken the form of a very beautiful young girl in a long grey cloak and a shower of beautiful brown hair. I watched her intently and as she bowed her fair head and knee at the Name of Names she assumed exactly the attitude and appearance of the angels that overshadowed with their wings the ark and the Mercy Seat. In the perpetual struggle between the powers and principles of good and evil the obeisance rebuked and put to flight an evil thought."

The City Council did its very best to support the Congress with a Mayoral Reception: "Some three thousand people were present and yet there was plenty of space to walk about in these noble rooms. We arrived at nine and left at midnight. There was a band, tea, coffee, ices, champagne cup, claret cup, sandwiches, and speeches." Altogether some 7,000 people attended this Congress. It was to be followed in 1877 by the centenary of the Bath and West Agricultural Society. Sadly, these celebrations were cut short when tragedy struck with the collapse of the footbridge at Widcombe, with fatal consequences.

The discovery of the full extent of the Roman Baths in 1880 focused national attention on the city and drew many visitors. A new mood of self-confidence possessed the Council, even to the extent of loosening the purse strings. This enabled the construction of the Concert Hall adjacent to the Pump Room and the extensions to the already magnificent Guild Hall (the locals' 18th-century riposte to the visitors' luxurious Assembly Rooms). Electric lights flickered on in the 1880s and telephones began to jangle.

To crown it all, Major Davis, the City Architect, designed and built the Empire Hotel. An unkind anecdote calls this building "Major Davis' Revenge". It is alleged that he designed it out of pique, having been unfairly prevented from winning the competition to house the Roman Baths. He had come up with a design restoring the original Roman vaulted roof: the Council, on which Major Davis had enemies, had, at the last moment, changed the rules to specify a building with no roof. Revenge or not, certainly the Empire's three curious gables (representing the rich man's castle, the poor man's cottage, and the villa of those in between), together with the building's height, do monopolise the city centre's sky line with their massive incongruity. Be that as it may, the completion of the Empire seemed at the time to symbolise a future of unstoppable progress and endless prosperity in a world dominated by a beneficent Empire on which the sun never set. Events, however, were to prove otherwise.

The Empire's complacent façade epitomised Victorian self-confidence, soon to be shattered by war.

9 War and Peace

Time is a continuum, and man's attempt to cut it up into manageable chunks called 'centuries' is, of course, an arbitrary business. Nevertheless it has its uses: certainly in the case of Bath the last three centuries do, as it happens, coincide with certain definite stages in the city's progress.

Bath's heyday as a centre for health tourism falls almost exactly within the 18th century, or rather the century from the 1688 on, when Queen Mary's dramatically felicitous immersion launched Bath as a fashionable resort, until the 1790s, when the Napoleonic War abruptly terminated its growth. The following century charts an ascent from poverty, social unrest and constitutional injustice, upwards to reform, progress and ever-growing prosperity.

What pattern can be discerned within the 20th century? It was surely the era when scientific discovery went critical and took off in a myriad directions and at an unprecedented pace. But it was also the century, in Western Europe at any rate, when man displayed his moral shortcomings as dramatically as he was exhibiting his technical precociousness. In the century's wars, great powers, evenly matched and employing every form of scientific innovation, could wreak fearful havoc upon each other. Previous conflicts after the Industrial Revolution had mainly been colonial wars, where Europeans incurred tiny losses compared to the terrible destruction they inflicted on their often primitively-armed opponents.

In Kitchener's 1898 campaign in the Sudan, for example, the Battle of Omdurman resulted in over 10,000 Sudanese deaths, compared to just 28 in Kitchener's army. True, the American Civil War and the Boer War had shown what might happen when well-matched modern armies clashed: but nothing had prepared Europeans for the carnage they could create if they set their minds to destroying each other. The Battle of the Somme exacted a toll of 600,000 German casualties and 614,000 French and British.

The holocausts that the fighting soon created came as a massive shock to a generation which had envisaged steady advances towards solving all mankind's problems through the application of science and technology. The smooth upward curve of progress and civilisation had plunged irrevocably. The blood bath in France reflected in the daily casualty lists posed pressing questions about the real nature of Western 'Christian' civilisation. For religious people, tying to retain their faith in a God of Love, the questions were phrased: "Where was God in all this? Why was the good not immediately triumphing? Was there some moral defect in the national life which had dragged down this punishment on them?"

In Bath, one place where these questions were being addressed was in the monthly publication, *Bath Abbey Notes*. Throughout the four long years of war the Rector, Prebendary Boyd, in his Rector's letter, wrestled and agonised over these issues. He harbours no doubts about the rightness of the Allies' cause, and therefore the necessity for the conflict; his certainties remain undiminished by the fearful sacrifices demanded. So he writes, in October 1914: "The progress of the War takes precedence of all other subjects. Alike for the Christian and the humane point of view War is terrible and horrible ... Only one thing could have produced the marvellous example of unanimity and loyalty which we are witnessing – the conviction and certainty of vast multitudes that truth and justice and righteousness are on the side of the Allies; and falsehood, oppression and arrogance on the side of their enemy." While his conviction does not waver, he is concerned to urge people to look to the integrity of their faith as their personal contribution towards purging the nation's life. He was, therefore, active in supporting the National Mission of Repentance and Hope launched by the Archbishops of Canterbury and York in 1916. The declared aim, as stated by the Dean of Wells, was that: "Through the Mission, God would say, you must have a better England". A preacher despatched from London delivered a week of special addresses, held, (rather optimistically since the month was November), in the open-air in Abbey Churchyard.

Throughout the war the congregation were urged to support the war effort in many ways – voluntary help at the military hospital, working parties for making bandages and, almost unbelievably, sandbags for the trenches (the group is congratulated on sending off three dozen!) Food parcels are despatched to prisoners of war, and the Abbey insures itself against a new threat – aerial attack – with an extra premium of £50. Bath opened its doors to many of the wounded, and the Abbey congregation played their part.

When finally the War shuddered to a halt, Bathonians spontaneously filled the Abbey for a service of thanksgiving. Boyd writes in December 1918 of the mounting excitement of the last four weeks of the War – "To have lived through such a great and wonderful time and not to have been powerfully affected by it, that would indeed be a shameful thing! How ought we to be affected? This experience ought at least to do these things; it ought to make us more regardful of God, more thankful, more prayerful, more humble".

Slowly the world creaked back to a peacetime economy. Bath suffered less from the aftermath of the War than did some other cities since it was less dependent on industry, relying more on the moneyed class of visitors. Bath's few factories had benefited from war production, but, come the peace, they turned their swords into plough shares, or rather their aircraft into furniture.

The inter-war years were a time of stagnation. A 1920 guidebook stresses as Bath's main advantage its remarkably low death rate; but if the city was in danger of becoming a genteel health farm, it still boasted no less than four 5-star hotels to its credit.

The Abbey's magazine of the period reflects the parochial concerns of a complacent society: it gives passing thanks for the relatively swift and peaceable end of the General Strike, but devotes much more space to the more pressing concerns of repairs to the flagpole, and the attempt to make the preacher audible by installing Marconiphone's 'voice amplifiers' and 'projectors' (but it was to be a further 74 years before the problems of the Abbey acoustics were finally solved!)

The approach of war in 1939 was heralded in Bath by an ominous event: the Pump Room Trio, with its fine record of continuity (it dates from Beau Nash engaging a "Band of Musick" in 1704), was suspended for the duration as an economy. The course of wartime Bath itself is fully documented in David and Jonathan Falconer's *Bath At War*.

The city housed some notable exiles and refugees, the most numerous, of course, being the Admiralty staff, hastily vacating London for the Empire Hotel. The Admiralty presence has continued to be a significant element in Bath's affairs, celebrated by the gift of the freedom of the city to the Royal Navy in Bath. Today the Abbey congregation is heavily infiltrated by former naval persons and in my more paranoid moments I sometimes wondered if we were run by some sort of naval mafia! Certainly one of my worst moments in the pulpit occurred when I was inveighing against Lord Nelson because of his support for slavery (he thought it was good for the economy and essential for providing manpower for the merchant navy). In mid-harangue I raised my eyes to the congregation only to confront the steely gaze of the First Sea Lord seated at the back of the Nave. I was subsequently forgiven when I invited him to read a prayer commemorating the Royal Navy's later role in suppressing the slave trade, at the opening of the Wilberforce exhibition.

An exotic and distinguished refugee was the Emperor Haile Selassie of Ethiopia, who entered into the life of the local community and was much respected. During his stay he became a member of the Abbey's congregation. When I went to Addis Ababa in 1983, I visited its Coptic Cathedral and noticed an unusual feature for an Orthodox Church – a row of military banners mounted aloft. I asked why this was and received the answer: "During the War our Emperor went to live in Bath in your country and saw banners like that in the church there. So he brought the idea back to us." There is some corner ...

More enduring links were forged through the presence of United States forces stationed in the locality, and now commemorated in the Abbey by the Stars and Stripes hanging in the South Aisle. It is good to record a number of recent encounters

The Stars and Stripes hanging at the back of the Abbey commemorates the presence of American forces in Bath during World War II.

with American visitors who first came to know the city in the course of their wartime service.

The conflict came most sharply home to the city, of course, on the nights of Saturday 25th and Sunday 26th April, 1942 – the Bath blitz. At that stage in the War, before the days of radio aids, night-time aerial navigation was a somewhat hit and miss affair. The R.A.F. were unable to pinpoint targets inland in Germany with any accuracy:

The scars of war are still visible in Bath. This building, next to Bath College, bears the marks of the 1942 bombing.

their only hope was to follow the coastline, the one landmark that could not be camouflaged or blacked out. Thus it came about that R.A.F. bombers delivered devastating attacks on the Baltic ports of Rostock and Lübeck – targets of little if any strategic importance but of considerable historical and aesthetic value. Hitler was furious at the effectiveness of these attacks and, in retaliation, launched the so-called Baedeker raids on cities meriting 4-stars in the guidebook of that name on account of the richness of their heritage. Bath was among the first victims: over 400 died and some 1,000 buildings were destroyed or seriously damaged in the two nights of repeated attacks.

The Abbey's Rector at that time, Archdeacon Selwyn, wrote shortly afterwards in his magazine letter about his reaction to those two terrible nights. He confessed that he had had to tear up the first draft, so full had it been of thoughts of revenge. "Who could have been out on those two grim nights, amidst the blazing homes and churches, with the dead, maimed and wounded lying all around, and the bombs still falling, without those feelings in one's heart? But hatred is really rather a poor thing; it uses up one's energies, blinds one's judgment, and does not get one very far ... The glory of Bath is now just dust and rubble, but the spirit of Bath and of those who came to help us was truly great."

His sentiments were echoed by the Diocesan Bishop, Bishop Underhill, who spoke at the funeral service at Haycombe, encouraging people to face the future with courage and without bitterness. He had personally taken part in searching the ruins of Walcot Church for the dead body of its Rector. Four other churches were destroyed in the bombing, including St James', and others were damaged. At St John's Roman Catholic Church, the two curates were standing in the Church porch watching events, when a bomb fell nearby. One was killed: the other, Monsignor Kelly, is now living in retirement at St John's Presbytery.

The Abbey was fortunate in losing only a part of its East Window. Fragments of the glass were collected, and were used shortly after the War when the window was rebuilt by the grandson of the original Victorian artist.

There are those alive today who were on duty as fire-watchers on the Abbey roof on those terrible nights. A month after the bombing, the *Bath Chronicle* published, as a sign of hope, a photograph of the first couple to be married in the Abbey, standing in the porch with the damaged window visible behind them. Fifty years on the picture was reproduced as the front cover of *Abbey News*. It reached the couple concerned, then celebrating their Golden Wedding in Kent. They were delighted to see themselves so miraculously rejuvenated.

A healing sequel to the blitz occurred 50 years later in 1992, when the City Council initiated a commemorative Sunday. There was to be a service at Haycombe Cemetery in the morning, where the dead lie in communal graves (their names are amongst all those listed in a beautiful Book of Remembrance kept in the Abbey). This morning service was to be followed by a second, held at the Abbey in the afternoon, and shared with a civic deputation from our twin city of Brunswick (Braunschweig). At the Abbey we insisted that while the morning service would properly look backwards in commemoration, the afternoon service should look forward in reconciliation. There were predictable fears and anxieties about this – "It's too soon– There'll be complaints". There were none; the service went forward most movingly and culminated in Bath's Mayor and Braunschweig's Lord Mayor shaking hands.

The success of this symbolic act of civic reconciliation produced a counter invitation two years later for myself, as Rector, to preach at a service in Braunschweig Lutheran Cathedral to mark the 50th anniversary of the bombing of that city. The two years that had separated the German bombing of Bath from our subsequent bombing of Braunschweig had seen the development of terrible air power and precision. Our bombing of Braunschweig caused ten times the number of deaths that Bath had suffered. Many of the dead were guest-workers, a euphemism for 'slave labourers', who were banned from using the citizens' air-raid shelters. The commemorative service faced me with the challenge of preaching perhaps the hardest sermon I have ever had to compose (not helped by the fact that it was planned to be delivered at a time to coincide with the R.A.F's arrival over the city in 1944 – 2.00 am).

What could one say? I prayed and preached. The congregation listened with close attention and much subsequent discussion ensued. The Cathedral's Dean, the Revd Joachim Hempel, had prepared for the event with a month-long lecture programme of public education on what were still sensitive issues in Braunschweig – What happened to that city's Jewish community? What was the role of the Gestapo in Braunschweig? and so on.

Challenged by Joachim's courage, we decided to invite him back a year later to preach at the Abbey's Civic Service marking the 50th anniversary of VE Day. It was a calculated risk, since clearly many veterans of the conflict would not take kindly to the thought of having a German preacher on this particular occasion. So it was a tense and not altogether friendly congregation that watched Dean Hempel mount the steps to the pulpit. (In that same pulpit Archdeacon Selwyn had placed a large radio set 56 years before, so that the congregation could hear Neville Chamberlain proclaim that war had been declared). With his first words Dean Hempel completely transformed the atmosphere. Echoing the declaration made by Germany's Confessing Churches just after the War, he said – "It was we Germans who were at fault. It was we who brought all this misery upon Europe". The reaction of the congregation was palpable; a sigh of relief ran through the pews.

Domprediger Joachim Hempel of Braunschweig Lutheran Cathedral plants an apple tree after the VE Day service in 1995.

After the service our visitor was roundly clapped when he planted a little apple-tree outside the South-east door of the Abbey. The tree is growing vigorously today and is backed by a text from the Book of Revelation, in which John describes the New Jerusalem. Through the centre of the city runs a river. On its banks trees are planted, "and the leaves of the trees serve for the healing of the nations".

"The leaves of the trees serve for the healing of the nations."

For many present on that day, the service marked a turning-point in their thinking about the War, and about Germany. For the Abbey it was the start of a fruitful interchange with our friends in Braunschweig Cathedral, within the wider link that the two cities enjoy.

This fifty-years-on piece of reconciliation had been preceded by another healing city link, actually inaugurated while World War II was still in progress.

A Dutch refugee from the city of Alkmaar, Eli Prins, then living in Bath, addressed Rotary and told them how people there were suffering under the Nazi occupation. This led to a wave of sympathy and much practical activity from 1942 onwards. The process was accelerated by Bath's own experience of *blitzkrieg*. A fund was formed and generously supported, so that at the very first opportunity after the liberation, money and a substantial collection of supplies were sent to Alkmaar. The U.S.A.A.F. flew the Dutch Mayor to Bath to be guest of honour at a special Alkmaar Week Ball held in the Pump Room. This was soon followed by regular exchanges of schoolchildren between the two cities. In the Town Hall in Alkmaar there stands a barrel-organ, painted in Dutch national colours, which once toured the streets of Bath every weekend to drum up support for the Appeal. The bond between the two cities continues with great vitality to this day.

Since 1945, Bath's only immediate experience of conflict has been the detonation of an I.R.A. device in The Corridor. Mercifully the only casualty was an abundance of plate glass. More recently Camilla Carr, from Bath, together with a friend, were kidnapped in Chechnya while working with a charity to help children orphaned by that war. Family and friends strove with determination and energy to keep their names in the public eye. As part of their campaign, they asked for a service of prayer to be held in the Abbey. This duly took place and was televised: extracts from the service were shown on Russian television, in the hope of touching someone with influence to help. It is good to record that Camilla and her friend John were finally released, and were subsequently married in Bath.

In our shrinking world, Bath has become something of a global crossroads. Our links stretch out in many directions. Most of the churches have their own overseas connections, and it is good to

An annual service of prayer and laying of a wreath commemorates the Far East Prisoners of War who did not come home. (Photo by courtesy of H.Tremblett)

remember an ecumenical effort that sent a convoy of clothing and other supplies for orphans to Romania. As a city we have many opportunities to offer friendship and, sometimes, practical help. The last century was marred and scarred by the two World Wars. Global peacemaking is still in its infancy: the United Nations has failed to prevent numerous conflicts since 1945 which have in total caused many more deaths than World War II. Perhaps the 21st century may be the Century of Peace. If so, Bath, already a cosmopolitan crossroads, will certainly have its part to play in the process.

10 Bath's Balance Sheet

We have traced Bath's growth from its simple origins as a hot spring welling up in a clearing, where the Celts came to worship such a mysterious manifestation of the deity Sulis. We have seen how the Romans came first to scoff at this numinous swamp, but stayed on to pray, after marrying up Sulis with the goddess Minerva. In time Aquae Sulis was to become a thriving leave centre for an army chilled to the bone by Britannia's cold climate. The Saxons inherited this legacy of grandeur but did not know what to make of it. It was left to the Church to provide a fresh focus for the town's life. The buildings erected for the Brothers of St Peter were to house Edgar's Coronation in 973, thus sealing the unification of the kingdoms of Mercia and Wessex.

Up to the Reformation first the Saxon monastery and then the great Norman cathedral were to give Bath its *raison d'être*, occupying a quarter of the city and dominating its economy. The two succeeding centuries of religious and constitutional struggle left Bath in the doldrums, with its new Abbey incomplete for half that time. A King's essay into alternative medicine and his Queen's conception of a child destined to become the Old Pretender launched Bath into its new prosperity as a health spa and gave that talented triumvirate – Beau Nash, Ralph Allen and John Wood – the opportunity they needed to transform the city. Then High Society discovered the seaside and Bath's fortunes ebbed, and partially foundered on the economic rocks of the Napoleonic Wars. Bath recovered in time to catch up with the 19th century just in time for the 20th century, aided by the rediscovery of the 1st century's Roman Baths. And the century just ended has seen two devastating wars, followed by the Cold War – each with its impact on Bath. It is ironic that it was President Gorbachev's declaration of peace which torpedoed Bath's defence establishment and caused a further economic shift away from defence and light manufacture into the world's fastest growing industry – tourism.

It is now time to make an assessment of where the city stands today and to draw up some sort of a balance sheet as we plan for a new future. As throughout this book, so here especially what follows is an entirely personal set of opinions – some would say idiosyncrasies and prejudices.

When training for the ministry, I underwent a scheme of preaching preparation called 'Bouquets and Brickbats'. A syndicate of six or so of us would sally out on a Sunday evening to some remote parish church in the Cambridgeshire countryside, where one unfortunate member of the group would mount the pulpit and attempt to amaze the (mercifully few) rustic parishioners with a display of wit and erudition. On the Monday morning the group would gather again over coffee and analyse the sermon. First of all everyone would feel obliged to offer a few insipid bouquets. Then the gathering got down to the serious business – the casting of brickbats at the preacher's efforts. Let us attempt a similar procedure with the city of Bath as it stands poised on the brink of the 21st century.

The first bouquet to land would undoubtedly be a compliment on the city's good housekeeping. Externally, the visitor is immediately aware of the work of the Parks Department in presenting 'Bath in Bloom' each summer, preceded before Easter by the glorious welcome of the daffodils lining the routes into the city. More permanently, however, the effects of skilful conservation of Bath's buildings are wonderfully evident. The last few decades have witnessed a face-clean of the mass of Bath stone – so beautiful and yet so fragile – which composes our architectural heritage. We are at least aware of the damage pollution causes even if as yet we have no effective solutions to prevent the problem arising.

I recall a sad morning spent in the city's archive looking at a series of photos of the Abbey's West Front, taken roughly every ten years or so over the past century. It was tragic to see the steady degradation of the West Front's carving over that period under the relentless attack of acid rain and the pollution released from the gas works upwind – now mercifully quenched. The skilled work of the conservation firm Nimbus has restored some detail to many of the sculptures, but even Nimbus was unable to bring back to life the heavenly host of angels looking down from the top of the façade. They are condemned to a shadowy, evanescent half-life (perhaps, it must be admitted, not totally unsuited to their status). The saintly figures below them, however, have taken on a new vigour.

When work began to conserve the West Front a particular question arose regarding the statue of St Philip. He stands on the north side, the topmost figure clutching the bread he brought to Jesus when confronted by the hunger of 5,000 followers. The original statue, however, had suffered badly from frost and wind and had lost its head and upper torso (my private name for what remained was 'the headless horror'). What were we to do – leave well alone or replace with a new statue? Our committee included six experts, representing English Heritage and five other conservation bodies. I consulted each expert in turn. With gravity and at suitable length they delivered their considered judgements – three in favour of replacement and three against! This confirmed my opinion of experts. With my casting vote I was able to ensure that contemporary skill should be represented on the west front. St Philip now holds high his head, while another work by the same sculptor takes shape down below.

The pollutant onslaught on this 500-year-old treasury of craftsmanship is happening to buildings across the city. It has to be checked. At least we are beginning to move in the right direction to conserve a city of such distinction. It is also a city with a historic core uniquely homogeneous in date and style, with the Abbey as the only medieval outsider amongst all the Georgian conformity.

If we are beginning to check the damage that has been caused by pollution, it is to be devoutly hoped that the deliberate damage caused by inept and unimaginative planning in the 1960s could not be repeated today. The wholesale destruction wrought in that decade has been chronicled in Adam Fergusson's indictment, *The Sack of Bath*. We have been brought to a sobering repentance for having permitted so much destruction of what could have been conserved and renovated, and for its replacement with such banal developments.

However, in the city's newer buildings there are signs of hope that may encourage us. The decision to pull down the Southgate centre and try again can only be good. The originality of the Seven Dials development gives us hope that next time we may get it right.

Most significant of all, as we contemplate the future, are the clear signs of a willingness to accept our destiny as a tourist mecca, and accordingly to set in place the right and appropriate steps for welcoming our visitors and sharing our heritage. A watershed

A sign of hope: the Seven Dials development.

was reached in 1979 when funds were made available by the city to develop the archaeological discoveries inaugurated by Professor Barry Cunliffe in the area of the Roman Bath and adjacent Temple. This made it possible for England's most significant Roman civic remains to be presented to millions of visitors and to enable them to access a civilisation that lies, in every way, just under the surface of our own. The Roman Baths complex had been a major unrealised asset for the city, picked over in the preceding two centuries but never explored properly until the last few decades.

In another lesser way too Bath has taken seriously the presenting of its past – in its ready reception of the numerous film crews queuing up to make travelogues, to shoot costume dramas, or to cash in on Bath's rich architecture. Bathonians now bat no eyelids if, on turning a corner, they come face to face with the world of Jane Austen or Joanna Trollope. Some years ago the south side of the Abbey was transformed into the outside of the House of Commons. A massive polystyrene wall, with inset wicket gate, was erected against the end of the transept. So skilful was this *trompe l'oeil* that even members of the Abbey's congregation, hurrying past, paused to wonder why they had never before noticed this feature. I was particularly delighted when the Archdeacon of Bath himself was fooled by this sham and alarmed by the apparent desecration of the Abbey.

Bath is unique. It is right that we should share its riches with the world; indeed it is essential for our economy that we do so. But the tragedy of tourism is that, if uncontrolled, it eventually kills that which it comes to see. How are we to preserve what is so precious while sharing it with nearly three million visitors each year?

Here, perhaps, we may be permitted a few brickbats. Some of our unresolved problems are obvious. A solution has not yet been found to the dilemma of limiting traffic in the city centre without converting that centre into a ghost town. Is it not time to take a closer look at the sort of scheme mooted a couple of years ago by a civil engineer in the *Bath Chronicle*? He proposed that the Recreation Ground should become a vast underground car-park, roofed over and returfed above so that its present sporting use could continue unabated. Such a development might absorb invisibly the entire demand for city centre passenger traffic, to the great benefit of the city's respiratory health. London has achieved a similar solution in Hyde Park: why not Bath? Some such radical way through must be found. If Perugia can leave its traffic at the foot of a cliff and bring its visitors to the top by a spectacular series of escalators, cannot Bath devise a similarly innovative scheme?

Banishing the infernal combustion engine from the centre while enabling easy access for passengers and other pedestrians would produce the greatest possible improvement in the city's physical environment. But the human environment is even more important. The visitor to Bath will be immediately struck by the number of homeless people squatting in doorways or boozing under the colonnades of the Abbey Churchyard. These people in many cases need skilled help and individual care. At present assistance is given through the excellent facilities of Julian House provided by the Bath Churches Housing Association in Manvers Street, and by other charities. Should there not be more positive moves by the local authority itself to steer folk off the streets and towards the right sort of care and assistance?

Higher standards and more imagination are needed to restore a city, which UNESCO has singled out in its entirety as a World Heritage Site, to its proper position in our national life. At the moment what can one say of a riverine city which makes attractive use of only a part of its river bank? Of a rash of new super-pubs but no central museum in a city with a fascinating history? Of a city with a vibrant musical life and a world-class music festival

Pulteney Bridge: this side – one of the glories of Bath ...

... this side – an eyesore

*Kingston Square: high aspirations once planned a Royal Forum here,
and later a grandiose approach to the city centre ...*
... Kingston Square today: the awful reality

but no purpose-built concert hall? It is sad to note that a recent survey of 17,000 *Guardian* and *Observer* readers put Bath behind Salisbury for the welcome it offers its visitors.

Part of Bath's problems lie in an apparent lack of clear direction resulting sometimes in seeming paralysis. We appear, for example, unable to limit the excessive number of tour buses, trundling round with half-a-dozen passengers at 20 mph, which do so much to clog the city's traffic flow. Nor does it seem feasible to emulate Taunton in licensing our buskers, so as to encourage the fun and the entertainment value provided by the 95% while curbing the cacophony and vulgarity of the 5% who let the city down.

Bath's buskers (with one or two exceptions) bring vitality and entertainment to the city centre: delightful African rhythm in the Abbey Churchyard.

If Bath is special, then this must be reflected in its local government structure. At present it is linked to other, quite different communities within the district of Bath and North East Somerset; does not the very infelicity of the title reflect the unworkability of its structure? Sometimes it seems that nothing can be undertaken in Bath that cannot be replicated in Norton Radstock, Keynsham and Midsomer Norton – which could provide a clear recipe for doing nothing!

Bath must be set free to be its true self. Only so can it work towards those standards of excellence that at present sometimes elude it. Much has been achieved in recent decades: more surely needs to be done to point the city towards its unique cultural heritage and its cosmopolitan future.

11 Soul Survivors

In *Roman Bath Discovered*. Professor Cunliffe gives a vivid account of the 1960s dig that led to the opening up of the Temple precinct adjacent to the Baths. He recalls the point when the bottom step leading up to the Temple's façade had just been uncovered: "worn by the tread of innumerable Roman feet. It was a satisfying moment. Standing on the step, 4.6 metres below the modern city, provided a rare occasion for evocative, rambling thoughts about what it would have been like to stand on this spot 1600 years earlier, what sounds, what light, what movements. Suddenly the illusion was shattered: from high above in the street a Salvation Army band began to play 'Hark, the Herald Angels Sing': it was Christmas Eve".

Professor Cunliffe is suggesting here that the sounds wafted down from above emanated from a quite different world from the one into which his imagination was leading him down below. And yet, of course, the Christian faith took root in Bath only a little while after the adherents of Sulis-Minerva built their Temple.

1600 years is a long time and the story of Christianity in Bath needs to be told and treasured. This impulse was the motive that led to the construction of the Abbey's Heritage Vaults in the cellars that lay adjacent to the Abbey on the South side. Originally they contained coal for the cottages above, huddled up against the Abbey's wall. Now, with the help of Bath City Council, they house one of Bath's most fascinating smaller museums, drawing over 20,000 visitors a year. The Vaults present something of the history of Bath's Christianity through the medium of the Abbey's own faith story. The museum has the added integrity of being located on the actual site of the history it relates: the woman's skeleton described earlier, still reverently contained within her stone coffin if now under thick glass, has been moved only a few feet from the spot where she was buried around the year 1200.

Our history is vital nourishment for us all, and Henry Ford was talking bunk when he denied that fact. For a historical faith, it is even more essential. It provides us with a springboard to launch us into the future: it is abused when it is used as a straitjacket to hold us back in the past. So let us draw together some of the threads of our story.

Out of the twilight of the Romano-Celtic world, it was the Christian community that made Bath once again a significant city and gave it a place in history as the site of our first Coronation. The Norman invasion led to the construction of John of Tours' cathedral and for the next 400 years Bath life revolved around Bishop and Prior. John of Tours, according to William of Malmesbury, was high-handed and arrogant towards the Saxon monks, whom he replaced with his own countrymen. Nevertheless, his vision was to make the monastery the hub of Bath's existence, the source of its economic wellbeing, a centre of worship, learning and healing.

As we have seen, King Henry VIII closed the monasteries to secure their assets and, for his own purposes, permitted a moderate version of the Reformation to develop, cuffing off Rome's jurisdiction. The effect of the Reformation was, above all, to democratise religion, putting a Bible in English into every man's hand and assuring people of their right of direct access to God.

The Age of Reason lowered the temperature of religious debate and put an end to the appalling distortion of Christianity which led people to persecute those who did not share their beliefs. The very nominalism of much 18th-century religion contributed to the new spirit of tolerance that was abroad: it is much easier to be tolerant if you lack strong convictions yourself.

The Age of Reason was challenged by the great revival movement of the second half of the 18th century. This recall to personal faith and commitment was to change the face of religion and to transform the morals of society as a whole. The Evangelical Revival has even been credited with sparing England from the wave of violent revolution that gripped our continental neighbours in 1848.

Higher standards of public integrity and the presence of men of moderation and Christian conviction within the Chartist movement all contributed to a greater sense of national cohesion than was enjoyed by some more polarised nations.

In Bath itself the 19th century saw the Churches in the lead in the movement towards universal education, and active in the improvement of medical services. A sad complacency, however, appears to have gripped the community when it came to public health. City pulpits seem to have been more preoccupied with the vices of the idle rich rather than with the plight of the helpless poor, condemned to live in insanitary squalor. The Churches no doubt had their own internal preoccupations – with putting up more buildings and, in the case of the Anglicans, with arguing the great disputes opened up by the High Church Oxford Movement. This Movement was both a sequel to the Evangelical Revival and a reaction against it. The Church of England was torn apart by the tension. I find it immensely encouraging to read the prediction of Dr Arnold of Rugby, delivered in 1851: "the Church of England as it now is no human power can save": what encourages me is the fact that we are still here.

The 1873 Church Congress must have had a unifying and rallying effect on all who took part. Nine years earlier a deeper note had been struck when Livingstone delivered his clarion call in Bath on the subject of slavery. His other major address during that visit to England had been given in Cambridge, where he appealed for more missionaries to consolidate the work in the areas he had pioneered. The Anglican response was the formation of the Universities Mission to Central Africa. From its work sprang, amongst other things, the formation of an indigenous Anglican Church in what is now Zambia. Today the Diocese of Bath and Wells is linked with this Church and a number of Bath congregations, including the Abbey's, participate actively in this link.

In pursuance of this link, Margaret and I visited Zambia in 1997. Our travels took us first to the town of Kitwe, in the copperbelt, where the church's seminary is situated – the Abbey's particular 'twin'. We were given a wonderful welcome by the staff, headed by the Principal. He was an expatriate Sudanese whom we knew from our time in Salisbury Diocese, which has a similar link with the Sudanese Church: what a wonderful multinational is the Christian Church.

After strengthening our bonds with the Seminary we headed south to Livingstone by the Victoria Falls, where the Zambezi forms the frontier with Zimbabwe. It was moving to discover Livingstone's statue gazing out across the mighty curtain of falling water. Unlike most statues from the colonial era he has not been thrown down. The Zambians appreciate his motivation and respect him enormously. In Bath his sole memorial is a pub in Oldfield Park.

The experience of spending two weeks in one of the world's poorest countries, where 25% of the population is H.I.V. positive, had a profound effect upon us. It was to flesh out my imagination when we became caught up in the Jubilee 2000 campaign.

Inevitably the history of Bath Christianity in the 20th century is the record of Christians struggling to respond to the needs of a community caught up in rapid change and, at times, dire emergency. The first decade saw the Church perhaps numerically stronger than it has ever been. Across the Anglican diocese vast numbers of clergy looked after 503 livings, their distribution in many cases having little regard to the current distribution of population. In 1904, 103 of these clergy had been in their parishes for 25 years or longer. In Bath a 1912 calculation estimated that 50% of all Bathonians were to be found in church on a Sunday.

Social concern is evidenced by the existence in the city of a branch of the Police Court Mission, precursor of the Probation Service, and an industrial training centre to help young offenders.

After the traumatic events of the 20th century and the technological changes which have transformed so much of life, the Churches in Bath today continue to enjoy a vigorous existence. We do not always heed that great dictum of Archbishop Temple: "The Church is the only institution that exists for the benefit of those who are not its members", but we do try. We have already mentioned the great work of Julian House (and now Barnabas House as well) and of the Genesis organisation in helping those living rough on the streets of Bath. It was a Christian impetus also that brought into being Dorothy House, our local hospice. Church members are heavily involved in these two areas of need, and in many other of those voluntary concerns which are one of the glories of our society.

Milton, slating the idle clergy of his day, wrote: "The hungry sheep look up, and are not fed". The situation now, we are told, is different: nowadays the sheep look fed up and are not hungry. Personally I do not believe this to be true. Along with all other activities demanding active participation, the churches have suffered numerical decline. Yet, if fewer in numbers and on average older than once we were, we are a leaner, fitter and far more active body than a few decades back. Bath churches see at least 10% of the population each Sunday, and a far higher percentage at Christmas and Easter.

At the Abbey, we welcome some 700 worshippers in the course of a Sunday, amongst them a good sprinkling of visitors from all over the English-speaking world. If our week by week ministry is to our regular congregation joined by Bath's visitors, we also serve the community as a whole by enabling people to bring their major concerns before God. Twenty or so carol services in December exemplify this process, but it is to be seen also in Remembrance Sunday Parades, the Bath Festival Service and many other one-off special occasions.

I recall how moving it was to stand in the pulpit on the night we marked the death of Diana, Princess of Wales. Above a packed congregation I could see out of the opened West doors to the great crowd stretching across to Stall Street, joining in the service via the external loudspeakers. At the conclusion of the service over 1,000 people filed in to light a candle.

The Churches of Bath are also much more united than only a short time ago. Over the 1600 years of Christianity in Bath, we have been divided for less than 500 years: now we are launched on a convergence course. All of us were heartened by the fact that, at the united service in Victoria Park on Pentecost Sunday 2000, held specially to mark the Millennium, all but three of Bath's 83 churches were represented.

Through the Churches Together in Bath network, we meet regularly with our ecumenical neighbours to discuss and to concert action. We fought, unsuccessfully, to Keep Sunday Special. Now it looks as if the forces of big business are massing once again to break down the regulations limiting Sunday shop hours to six. Once again we may see big national chains of stores, who should know better and behave more responsibly, prepared to break the law as a means of changing it.

Christians united more successfully to campaign for Jubilee 2000, which aims to bring about the cancellation of unrepayable debts owed by Third World countries. The campaign is today's equivalent of Wilberforce's crusade against slavery, two centuries back. Progress is being made by Jubilee 2000 and it is good to record our own government's initiative in urging this move upon the world's wealthiest nations. Bath Churches have been vigorously active in this campaign.

We have not yet found the right way to relate corporately to the other faith communities in Bath – Muslim, Jewish, Bahai, Hindu, Sikh. If sharing in worship cannot be undertaken without compromise or unreality, this should only renew our determination to develop some other form of interfaith forum where we can meet and gain mutual understanding.

Wilberforce's campaign against slavery is echoed in today's Jubilee 2000 campaign, supported by many Bath churches. (Photo by courtesy of the Wilberforce House Museum, Hull)

This little book, as was hinted at the start, has been very much one person's view of Bath from an unusual viewpoint – through the Abbey's windows. This chapter takes its title from an annual celebration of the faith for young people: over 5,000 of them, drawn from Bath, from all over this country and beyond, have just been sharing a week of music, seminars, Bible study, great fun and wholehearted worship at the Bath and West Showground. The faith is as alive and well today as it was when Annianus turned his baleful gaze on the Christians whom, amongst others, he darkly suspected of lightening his purse, some 1650 years ago. Christianity runs like a golden thread down through Bath's history, enriching, inspiring, life-giving.

A great figure from Bath's Christian past is echoed in a Millennium initiative at the Abbey. A series of annual lectures has been inaugurated, dedicated to the memory of William Wilberforce, on the theme of 'the application of Christian principles to public life'. An inspiring first address was delivered in June 2000, by The Rt. Hon. Chris Patten, on the needs of the Third World.

Two works of art are being added to the Abbey also in this Millennium year. Outside, confronting the passers-by, is a vital figure of Christ risen from the dead and gloriously alive. It is the work of a sculptor who himself came to new life through the faith he discovered, Laurence Tindall, who has already contributed to Bath the figure of Julius Caesar overlooking the Baths; St Philip on the Abbey's West Front; and the Loaves and Fishes outside his own church of St Philip and St James, Odd Down.

Inside the Abbey a vast frontal, created by Jane Lemon and the Sarum Group, adorns the High Altar, depicting a fountain-spring of crystal water. It recalls the vision of John in Revelation, Chapter 22, of "the river of the water of life, bright as crystal, flowing from the throne of God and of the Lamb, through the middle of the street of the city. On either side of the river is the tree of life ... and the leaves of the tree were for the healing of the nations."

"The river of the water of life, bright as crystal, flowing from the throne of God."

12 Pilgrim's Progress

We have peered out at Bath's fascinating history from the vantage point of its most significant building. An Abbey-eye view may not be a bad way to gain some insight into the city with which it has been so closely enmeshed through the centuries. It may be helpful, finally, to add a personal note to provide a glimpse of the man behind the binoculars.

When the time came for me to leave my previous post at Salisbury Cathedral I remarked, rather grumpily, to Margaret: "Whatever church we go to from here is certainly not going to be a great heap of stone with a high musical tradition and a financial appeal hanging over it." God heard, and smiled; it is highly dangerous to make such remarks in His hearing. Inexorably I found myself drawn to the post at Bath Abbey

The reasons for my reluctance were clear. Like all well-brought-up Evangelicals, I had nourished, during my early years in the ministry, an abhorrence of large, grand churches because, so we believed, the building got in the way of the Gospel. If you could worship God in a field, why bother with a large and costly edifice? So ran the creed of what is sometimes referred to as 'Elsan theology'. This view had been somewhat tempered by seven years at Salisbury Cathedral. I had come to Salisbury from a Surrey parish with one modern church and one picture postcard, ancient parish church. In the modern church worship was none too formal and God was definitely in our midst. The temptation to be 'matey with the Almighty' was ever-present. By contrast, the Cathedral, with its massive dimensions and minutely regulated worship, came as a douche of cold water. One was forcibly reminded that God is "high and lifted up", as well as accessible and present amongst us – the polarity known to theologians as 'transcendence and immanence'. So it was that on leaving Salisbury I hankered to return to the warmth of a close Christian fellowship.

My anxieties about a high musical tradition stemmed from the unfair distribution of God's gifts within our family, whereby all the musical appreciation had by-passed me and headed straight for Margaret. I could view the arcane mysteries of classical church music only with a reverent agnosticism. The prospect of presiding over a church with a cathedral-standard choir and two choral services each Sunday frankly appalled me with the thought of my own inadequacy. The further prospect of hosting some 50 musical events a year over and above our worship seemed to be a sick joke.

As for the financial appeal, I had just emerged from the life of a Cathedral which had been chasing £16m for some years. Though not closely involved with the fundraising, I had seen the distortion of the church's ministry that this quest had cause. Along with my Cathedral post as Canon Treasurer, I held, too, a diocesan post as Adviser on Mission; I now faced the prospect of being buried alive in a stone tomb of maintenance.

There was a further reason why Bath Abbey in particular looked like an alarming prospect. I would be following on from Prebendary Geoffrey Lester's 30-year incumbency, which had inevitably defined for his congregation what the Christian ministry was all about. His strength of character, preaching gifts and pastoral compassion had etched themselves indelibly onto the Abbey community. He would be a hard act to follow.

It was, therefore, only after a considerable amount of arm-twisting – divine and human – that I accepted the post of Rector, and approached my Induction Service in March 1990. My confidence was not increased when, coming across to Bath for the rehearsal of the service, I was confronted by a hostile crowd advancing on me and shouting: "Out! Out! Out!" It was only later that I discovered that this demonstration was a reaction to the City Council's debate that evening on the poll tax.

It was not until the night of the Induction itself, during the preliminary paperwork in the Vestry, that I found that I was also expected to become Vicar of St James. My anxious expostulations were soothed when somebody murmured in my ear: "Don't worry. Hitler dropped a bomb on St James, and what's left of it is buried under Littlewood's. It'll give you no trouble at all."

The next few years were a steep learning curve for me. We found a warm welcome and discovered that most people well understood that the Abbey must move on. There were, of course, occasional hiccups. Just a few weeks after my arrival the *Bath Chronicle* rang up to say that a lady had written to the paper complaining about some minor change I had made to the order of service and offering to raise a fund to send me back to Salisbury: would I like the right of reply? I duly thanked the lady for her generous suggestion but regretted that it had come too late, as I had already fallen in love with Bath.

It was clear that money would have to be raised to carry through the conservation of the West Front, for which a planning group had been set up by my predecessor. With a sinking heart I suggested that we should spend a year looking at and costing out the Abbey's total needs, and should then go for the much larger sum that would be needed. In this way six projects were identified, and our best guestimate suggested £2.5m for a campaign that was to be called 'Bath Abbey 2000'.

Learning from Salisbury's exhausting experience of fund-raising without outside professional help, we decided to make use of such a firm with a good track record. It was a bad moment, nevertheless, when we paid up a six-figure fee in advance, with no guarantee that we should raise a penny. We need not have feared. The fundraiser assigned to us, a committed Christian, applied himself with energy and integrity.

It was now essential that we should appoint the right person as our Treasurer for the campaign. This problem was much on my mind, even on my day off, when we dropped down to Bathampton village for a pub lunch at *The George*. There I found a former banker, Alec Ritchie, who had recently come to Bath and joined the Abbey, and who was now sitting in the pub, immobilised with a leg in plaster. Encouraged by his inability to flee, I approached him and asked him to be our Treasurer; fortunately for us he had little option but to agree. He served the Abbey wonderfully well in the ensuing years, up to his death this August.

A pyramid of covenants from the congregation together with the wholehearted participation of the Friends of Bath Abbey yielded an astonishing total of £1.25m. We could now look others in the eye and ask for their help. Bath City Council, industry and a large number of trusts and individuals of good will carried us forward. Of course the goal-posts had moved with the years and the revised target was now £4m. We made it with the help of two large grants of lottery money to aid the rebuilding of the organ to international standard, and the cleaning of the interior. By then the work on the West Front, the relighting of the interior, and the construction of the underground Heritage Vaults had already been finished. The final project, the repair and cleaning of the Abbey's north side is approaching completion as I write. It was a happy

The Prince of Wales honours the Abbey with a visit to commemorate the successful conclusion of Bath Abbey 2000.

day in the summer of 1999 – the quincentenary of the present Abbey Church – when we welcomed our patron, Prince Charles, to a celebratory visit and service of thanksgiving.

Throughout the fundraising campaign hardly a coffee cup was raised and not one box of jumble was sorted in the cause. The direct approach to give sacrificially and sensibly through use of covenants respects both the cause and the donor. It was a particular source of thanksgiving that our normal Abbey giving was unaffected by Bath Abbey 2000; indeed, in response to a diocesan appeal, our level of giving actually doubled. At the same time we continued to honour our pledge to give away one tenth of our annual income to missions and charities.

Bath Abbey 2000 proved to be a uniting challenge for the Abbey and not the idolatrous worship of sticks and stones that, in my worst moments, I had feared. The whole effort mobilised us and thawed us out in surprising ways, and led to a remarkable spin-off in terms of greater involvement. In our worship, lay people now began to read lessons, lead the prayers and assist in administering the Holy Communion. A group of Pastoral Assistants was selected and trained. A large team was formed to be responsible for the Christian nurture of our children. An encouraging postscript to Bath Abbey 2000 was a separate campaign to raise £75,000 so that we could employ a youth worker for three years. The sum was raised for this Millennium project, and there are now some 80 young people within the Abbey family who are being shown the Christian way.

I have learnt much during the past eventful ten years. I have found that God need not be remote when worshipped in a magnificent church. I have come to recognise afresh that church music, in many styles and at different levels of brow, is a vibrant carrier-wave for God's communication with us. Throughout my ten years I have valued greatly the Abbey's music with its pipe organ and three choirs: the Abbey choir of men and boys; the Evening Choir; and now the Girls' Choir, a great enrichment for the 9.15am service.

The Abbey's future: members of the Girls' choir enjoying the snow.

I have learnt, too, that a great building, far from being a hindrance to preaching the gospel, may actually convey the good news, both subliminally by the impact of the architectural statement and overtly by various forms of proclamation. What speaks loudest, of course, is the quality of welcome that greets the visitor from all who work within the Abbey. There is a place, too, for the Bookshop and for the video showing the Abbey as a body of believing men and women. We have already mentioned the powerful symbolism of Christian art. In needlecraft, the Sarum Group challenges us with their screen portraying Alphege's martyrdom, and with the river of life frontal. The Friends' generosity has also enabled us to add their Gethsemane Chapel frontal, with its design speaking of peace and light beyond suffering and sacrifice. It is the Friends, too, who commissioned Laurence Tindall's Risen Christ, taking form under his chisel outside the Abbey's south-east door.

Being Rector of Bath Abbey is a task both disintegrating and fascinating. One is torn between the roles of conservationist, charged with caring for a slice of the nation's heritage; of tourism promoter, looking after Bath's second most visited building; of concert-hall manager, financial director and fundraiser. All this, of course, is grafted onto the normal priestly vocation to preaching, teaching, pastoral care, daily worship and prayer. Allied to this is the chairing of innumerable committees, and many hours of office work.

Mercifully, in every area there is a team of committed people, some paid but most volunteers, all united in a common cause. Some 180 volunteers are involved in the weekday ministry to our visitors alone. Through their dedicated efforts some third of a million visitors each year are confronted with the reality of a living faith and a caring church. In all this work I have been blessed with much support and friendship from many people, headed by a remarkable succession of churchwardens. My clergy colleagues over these years, latterly women as well as men, have each contributed an array of gifts and talents. All have been, fortunately, both long-suffering and good-humoured.

Various images describing the Church are provided in the New Testament and by successive generations – The Vine; The Bride; The Body; The Sheepfold; The Living Stones; The Family. Best of all, for our day, perhaps, is The Pilgrimage – a company of friends heading towards the same destination but at their own pace, constantly being joined by others along the way.

Two factors had caused me personally to join the Pilgrimage – the lies of government ministers during a particular crisis; and, on a later occasion, the likely disapproval of my university tutor. As a young man the spectacle of the government being caught out in lying about the Suez operation shattered my security, as someone who had thought that God was certainly British, probably from south of the Watford Gap, and likely to vote Tory.

Subsequently the challenge delivered by an evangelist at a university mission led me into a wilderness in which I knew that Jesus was indeed the Son of God, alive and accessible; yet at the same time I could not bring myself to trust myself to him. This state of paralysis came to a head one morning when I had to deliver up an essay to my tutor at noon. The internal debate prevented my writing a word. In the end I knelt down and said: "Lord, I give in, but please let me get something down on paper". It was a terrible essay but I delivered it with a glad heart. As I ran up the High Street with it I noticed for the first time the sum shining on the gold cross on the University Church.

The Pilgrimage that began that day has led me through many curious ways. Very often I have strayed from the path and gone off on my own; yet somehow one always gets drawn back again. In recent years Margaret and I have been much involved in leading

The power of pilgrimage: Abbey members follow the Via Dolorosa in Jerusalem

literal pilgrimages to Jerusalem and elsewhere. To walk in the actual places where He walked is to furnish the imagination for the rest of one's days. Yet the real pilgrimage must be undertaken right here, at home. Bath's pilgrimage began, as we have seen, back in Roman times. Throughout the long centuries the Abbey's congregations, within the whole body of Bath Christians, have handed on the previous legacy of faith.

My ten years in Bath up to my retirement this year have been spent in that joyful company. I have learnt so much from my Bathonian fellow-pilgrims, both about Christian living and about Christian dying: they have my profound gratitude.

There is a moment in *Pilgrim's Progress* when Christian and his companion, lost on a high plateau, meet some shepherds who lend them a telescope:

> Then said the Shepherds one to another, 'Let us show to the Pilgrims the gates of the Celestial City, if they have the skill to look through our perspective glass'. Then they essayed to look, and they saw something like the gate and also some of the glory of the place.

Perhaps occasional glimmers of that glory may be seen within the life of our own city.

Retired – or re-tyred for a new stage of the journey?

Acknowledgements

The classic history of Bath Abbey was written by John Britton in 1824 and republished with additions by R.E.M.Peach, describing Kemble's restoration, in 1887.

Of contemporary books about Bath and the Abbey's place within it there is a cornucopia. For erudition and entertainment I would single out two by Professor Barry Cunliffe, *Roman Bath Discovered* and *The City of Bath. John Wood: Architect of Obsession* by Tim Mowl and Brian Earnshaw helps us understand Bath's 18th-century flowering, while Trevor Fawcett's and Stephen Bird's *Bath* gives us an excellent overall history. Dr John Wroughton's *A Community at War* depicts Bath in the Civil War period. The series of annual lectures, delivered under the auspices of the Friends of Bath Abbey, chronicle the development of the Abbey and its predecessors. A paper by Linda Jones, the Administrator of the Abbey Vaults, on 'The Abbey over the Last Millennium' adds much vivid detail.

To all the above I would express my gratitude, and to my wife, who spent many midnight hours typing up my manuscript.

Richard Askew was born in 1935. After National Service with the Royal Artillery in the Egyptian Canal Zone and a Classics degree at Oxford, he married Margaret and spent two years with the British Council in Sudan. Then, drawn to ordination, he taught for a year at Newquay Grammar School before training for the ministry at Ridley Hall, Cambridge. Curacies in Chesham, Bucks and Mossley Hill, Liverpool were followed by five years as student chaplain at St Aldate's, Oxford before moving to be Rector of Ashtead, Surrey from 1972 to 1983. He then spent seven years as Canon Treasurer at Salisbury Cathedral and Missioner in Salisbury Diocese. He became Rector of Bath Abbey from 1990 until his retirement in July 2000.